MW00427243

DOWN SOUTH JUSTICE

Animal Rescue in the Deep South

DAVID COWARDIN
AWARD-WINNING JOURNALIST

Illustration and Design by Matthew Olin | matthewolin.com

First Printing: December 2015

ISBN: 0692579141
ISBN-13: 978-0692579145

DEDICATION

For Sadie
(Fort Smith Chocolate Lab)

ACKNOWLEDGMENTS

Thank you to my entire family for your endless support and guidance, and to my friend Joe for joining me on this wild adventure.

OTHER ACKNOWLEDGMENTS

Animal Allies, Lorna Aho, Cloquet Friends of Animals, Nancy Altena, AVRAL, Brian Batista, Carol Bement, Mani Berti, Terry Blair, Richard Burgess, Paige Calhoun, Jeff Cerise, Garland Clarke, Bill Cowardin, Kati Cowardin, Lewis and Eustis Cowardin, Ted Cowardin, Carol Crocker, Darren Danielson, Jen Drier, Hannah Rey Dunda, India Erb, Fran Fields, Robbie Fitzgerald, Brandt Garrison, Kim Gentry, Emily Haavik, Lisa Hansen, Ryan Hanson, Lee Harrington, William and Dee Hartley, John Hatcher, Kim Hyatt, Lisa Johnson, Chris Julin, Glenn Kellahan, Brenda Knutson, Peter Knutson, Richard Koerner, Rachel Kraft, Brenda Lafontaine, Dayna Landgrebe, Ingrid Law, Dr. Leonard, The Leonard Family, Pam Leonard, Rachel Leonard, Paul Lundgren, Greg Mahle, Adam Meyer, Bonnie Miller, Tim Miller, Rod Moody, Sandra Nathan, Don Ness, Northland's Newscenter, Karin Newstrom Photography, Jennifer Dial Nolan, Ericka Olin, Matthew Olin, Joe Olivieri, Joseph Olivieri, Mario Olivieri, Rhonda Parker, UMD Beta Lambda PSI, Leavellwood Ranch, Austin Dog Rescue, Carl Sauer, UMD Statesman, Kaci Stokley, Scott Stone, Sonya Smith, Cynthia Sweet, Bobbi Taylor, Emily Thompson, Zach Vavricka, Tina Watson, WDIO-TV, Pat Webb, Wheels4Paws, Javalyn Wilson, Catherine Winter, Dena Yrjana

TABLE OF CONTENTS

INTRODUCTION

WHEN I RESCUED LENNY LOU, a lab/pit mix from Alabama, I had no idea what dog ownership would be like. I also didn't know Lenny had skin mites that would require me to dip her in acid baths, which ultimately led to Lenny's fear of water as a puppy.

I live in Duluth, Minnesota, and spend the majority of my free time near water: fly fishing and kayaking the tributaries of Lake Superior and paddling the Boundary Waters Canoe Area, a federally protected wilderness area in the Superior National Forest. I love water and now owned a dog that wanted nothing to do with it.

When Lenny was about a year old, I took her to the Lester River, where my fiancé, Dena, and I would jump from high cliffs into a deep pocket of water and bathe in the cold current. While Dena was playing with Lenny near the river, I climbed to the top of a cliff to take my first jump.

"Lenny!" I called down to my water-wary pup.

Lenny cocked her head at a 90-degree angle, curious as to why I was perched on a cliff above the river.

Then, I jumped, and on my way down, could see Lenny leap into the water, paddling awkwardly toward the middle of the river. When I emerged from my plunge, Lenny was circling me and pawing at my back, trying to rescue the man who rescued her.

Since then, Lenny has joined me on multiple trips to the Boundary Waters and has learned to jump from docks to retrieve sticks. She's also sat in my kayak as I paddled through rapids and over ledges. She still hates taking baths, but we're working on that.

I will never forget the day Lenny overcame her fear of water, because it was the first time I understood that dog ownership, isn't ownership at all. It's companionship. It's family.

I rescued Lenny after producing the documentary, "Roots of Rescue," which unveils the plight of animal rescuers in Alabama.

This book is an uncensored, intimate telling of those stories, recalling the journey of two photojournalists embedded in the American South, following a network of animal rescuers. Some carried badges and investigated under official capacity; others were vigilantes, taking the law into their own hands.

Justice, to the men and women we followed, had nothing to do with the law. Their form of justice was a different brand, a down south justice.

PART ONE
"I SHOT RIGHT AT THE BASTARDS"

THERE IS A GUN ON ALMOST EVERY SIDE TABLE AND NIGHTSTAND in her house and 40 rescue dogs howling from runs and kennels in her backyard.

Bonnie Miller is making a last stand in rural Greene County, Alabama. "The crazy lady on the hill" is pushing 60 and still investigating animal cruelty against her better judgment because "somebody's gotta do it."

Armed with a revolver, badge, and store-bought CSI hat, Bonnie noses her SUV down dirt roads in Alabama's rural ghettos, looking for signs of dog fighting. She always finds something.

Joe Olivieri and I were sitting in Bonnie's breezeway on fold-out lawn chairs waiting for the humidity to break. A gibbous moon hung in the night sky, crickets chirped a chorus with howling dogs, and mosquitoes emerged from the woods. Everything was hot and sticky. Nothing about the scene was spectacular. Nothing was special.

I slouched back in my chair and lifted my arms to air out my sweaty armpits. It had been days since my last shower. A soap container hung mockingly from the rearview mirror of the 25-foot RV we borrowed from Joe's grandfather. It had no water or air conditioning, and it smelled like old marijuana and sultry ballsack. But, it was home.

I could hear Bonnie flip on a blender inside the house, mixing us drinks.

Joe gave me a look that he's given me before, one that said *how the fuck did we end up here?*

Then the screen door swung open and Bonnie walked out with a sweating pitcher of pina colada. She poured us drinks in plastic cups and we debriefed on our first day in the field with her.

It was pathetic. Heaps of garbage burned in yards everywhere we went. Dogs lay dead in ditches with rotting gun shot wounds ... maggots occupying their insides. It was a real shit hole, a third world country hiding in the swamps of our nation. Overlooked and forgotten.

We followed Bonnie as she kicked up dust in neighborhoods where drug dealing and dog fighting were ubiquitous. Bonnie normally refused interviews with journalists but figured, "what the hell." A couple of college grads with cameras certainly can't make the situation any worse, and at least this way she would have some company and backup in the field.

Bonnie refilled her cup to "take the edge off" and reached down to pet a jumpy rescue dog she adopted. Then she repeated something she told us multiple times throughout the day: "The people in this county, they just don't give a damn," she said. "Not a damn."

She's right. Nobody gives a damn. Not the people in rural ghettos, not the law enforcement, and not the people insulated in nearby cities. Heck, Bonnie barely gives a damn anymore. She's been abandoned and left to fight a war on her own.

According to state law, every county in Alabama is supposed to have an animal shelter and animal control officer. Greene County, however, has Bonnie and her husband, Tim. Their property stands as the de facto shelter, with Bonnie the officer and Tim the financer. The operation has absorbed their retirement fund and at times, threatened their marriage.

You can see it in Bonnie's eyes as the sun goes down and her transitional lenses unveil more of her emotion: agony, stubbornness, and fearful pride. She's the embodiment of the dogs she rescues. But nobody is coming to rescue her because nobody gives a damn.

Tim returns home from work late. He cleans shit from kennels and helps Bonnie with whatever unique situation is playing out.

On this particular night, the scene involved a pit bull that had been starved and tied to a rope for so long that the rope started cutting through the dog's neck. An embedded collar, as it's called, is a clear sign of gross neglect and will turn your stomach inside out. Mr. Leroy, the dog's owner, can barely wipe his own ass. Could be drugs. Could be stupidity. Bonnie doesn't give a damn what it is, because either way, Mr. Leroy left his dog at the end of a rope in his backyard, rotting in its own piss and blood, and not for the first time.

Joe and I turned our cameras on as Bonnie and Tim devised a plan to stick the dog with a needle and inject an antibiotic.

Tim threw a treat in the back of its kennel, the dog turned its back, and then Bonnie opened the cage and stuck the dog in the rear. Bonnie and Tim: practiced and precise. It was clear they had done it before.

The cement slab in the breezeway started to cool. I kicked my shoes off and set my feet down, realizing how dirty I was as my feet released heat that condensed on the cold cement.

Bonnie was explaining to Joe and I just how real the war was. She told us how dog fighters will call her house to see if she's home. If she answers, they know it's safe to fight their dogs. It happens all the time and because Bonnie is the only person in the county investigating animal cruelty, the strategy works. But dog fighters don't want that burden; they want Bonnie gone.

Bonnie recalled an occasion when a pair of pit-bull fighting thugs parked their car at the end of her driveway, bumping their rap music. Taunting her.

Bonnie was in her yard and could see them through the bushes.

"I grabbed my shot gun and fired at 'em," she said.

"You mean you fired a warning shot in the air?" I asked.

"I shot right at the bastards," she was quick to respond. "And I hope I hit 'em."

As I watched Bonnie sip her drink and stare out over her yard of dog kennels, I realized that my life, the one I knew prior to parking the RV in Bonnie's driveway, was completely insular and adolescent, and about to change in ways I could only imagine.

THE FIFTH ESTATE

THE ROAD TO ALABAMA BEGAN IN A SMOKE-FILLED APARTMENT in Duluth, Minnesota's Hillside neighborhood.

Joe and I sat at opposite ends of his dining room table passing a bottle of port wine, trying to understand the meaning of life and how we could avoid becoming yet another casualty of capitalism. As recent college graduates, we were in that period of rebirth, trying to find new direction. Trying to find ourselves.

We hoped to discover an agreeable answer before the booze shifted our conversation to a more spacy realm.

We recalled events in our lives that brought us together. For me, the story began during my sophomore year of college at the University of Minnesota.

"A kid just pooped on your floor."

The waterpark manager squeezed through a crowd of tourists to the arcade display desk to notify me of a sanitation emergency.

"Since you're not trained to handle hazardous waste, I will have one of my lifeguards clean it up," he said with a wink.

I smirked and refocused my attention on a wet and pudgy kid trying to decide what to trade his 2,000 tickets for.

"This gun is 1,500 tickets," I pointed to a plastic toy on the mirrored wall behind me. The boy mumbled under his breath, uninterested in my suggestion.

I caught a glimpse of myself in the mirrored wall, devoid of life and wearing a melon-colored shirt that read "Fun Team" on the back.

Fuck me, I thought, before turning around to a fuming hotel guest wearing flower-printed board shorts and a tank top.

"What the hell is this? I want a refund! This toy is crap!" he barked.

"Unfortunately I can't refund on toys that have already been opened," I replied, examining the opened packaging and giving him a rehearsed response straight from the 'Fun Team' guide.

"Are you fucking kidding me?" he went off in a series of expletives, slamming the toy down in front of me, shattering plastic parts across the desk, while his son was probably shooting down a waterslide, forgetting the toy ever existed.

Normally, I ignored protocol and offered a refund, but this guy was a real asshole so I decided to use what little power I had as an arcade attendant.

"Look, you paid for your kid's entertainment, not that cheap piece of plastic," I told him. "Take it up with the kid in China working the assembly line, not me."

"I want to talk to your manager!"

And he did.

Joe slid the bottle of port wine across the table and I refilled my cup. I wasn't telling him the arcade story, just thinking about it and reliving the agony.

That's how we communicated. In silence over a bottle of wine, a campfire, or whatever was available. We would get lost in our respective nostalgia and occasionally blurt out some sort of prophetic insight on life—what little we knew about it.

Somehow we always managed to stay on the same page.

As the arcade thinned out, I was left standing behind the desk staring idly at blinking lights, choking on the smell of poop and carpet cleaner.

I slid a copy of the Duluth News Tribune across the Plexiglass desk and read the headline: 'Exercise ball-slasher sentenced to a year at NERCC.'

A man with a history of mental illness was satisfying his fetish of popping large exercise balls by breaking into fitness centers in Duluth. Over the summer, the media dubbed him the "Ball Slasher," a nickname that resonated quickly across Minnesota newswires.

Poor bastard, I thought. The media boosted their ratings, but at the expense of a mentally ill man and his family.

A month earlier, I sat in on editorial budget meetings at the Duluth News Tribune. As an intern, I was responsible for covering city news.

The internship started as an unpaid, 40-hours-a-week gig, but after human resources noticed our articles printed on the front page, they decided to pay us but cut our time in half. I could use the rent money, but would have rather built up extra clips for my resume.

The morning of my review was the morning after my 21st birthday. I threw up stomach bile into the toilet, brushed my teeth, put on a nice shirt and drove to the Tribune with a splitting headache.

The newsroom looked like a burnt forest, completely bare of life with the exception of a few lingering trees standing in stark contrast to the charred earth, similar to certain areas of the Boundary Waters north of Duluth.

There were more empty cubicles and fewer reporters than ever before. There was a shared anxiety, a *who-is-next* mentality that kept reporters sharp and editors spinning out ball-slasher-like headlines. There was a man in a glassed-in office applying for jobs in bigger markets, and there was me, a 21-year-old kid trying to navigate a world of new media, a lowly intern trying to get a leg up on the competition, switching between a 'Fun Team' polo and a button-down shirt.

I was walking into an industry deprived of oxygen, and much like that burnt forest, in a period of regrowth. I could hear the 100-year-old printing press moan like an old dog stirring in his sleep as I was led into a conference room for my review. Across the table sat the city news editor and managing editor.

"Do you remember your last story?" the city news editor asked.

She explained how she had to change my story after submission because a quote, according to my source, was incorrect. She never asked my side of the story or considered the validity of the source's argument. I was the intern. I was wrong.

"You ask too many questions," she said, telling me I should have taken more initiative instead of relying on her as a mentor.

It's a fucking internship, can't I ask questions? I thought as I cleared the bitter taste of purged stomach bile from my throat.

The managing editor cut in to calm the waters, telling me that I was pleasant to work with but needed more experience.

"Maybe some day you will prove us wrong," he cut in.

Fuck him.

I drove home and slept off the hangover of my internship.

I took a small sip of port wine, letting it pool on my tongue, and looked across the table at Joe who was licking small squares of paper, wetting them before rolling a joint.

I didn't have to ask him what he was thinking. During the summer of my internship, Joe was traveling the West Coast in his 1984 Westphalia camper van, facing his fear of traveling alone without money. He relived those memories every time he sought answers to life's persistent questions of being.

Solitude, "van life," he would say. And that's all he had to say. His face told me the rest: roadside van repairs, headstands against a dessert sunset, helpful strangers, the salty and sunny ocean, Kerouac, redwoods, breathing, living.

"Kill all irrational fear," Joe told himself repeatedly, bouncing along in Lola, the rusty orange camper van—the vehicle of his rebellion.

I swallowed my wine and felt a buzz come on. Then I replayed what the Tribune editor told me: "Maybe some day you will prove us wrong."

What did he mean? What was his point? I kept repeating it to myself, sipping more wine until drifting off into a numbing stalemate with my conscience.

That statement hung over me like Samuel Taylor Coleridge's albatross: a burden and saving grace. I knew if I killed it, it would be deprived of its purpose to lead me toward self-awareness. So I stayed angry, focused.

That year I became the editor in chief of our school's weekly newspaper and Joe became the managing editor.

The first year Joe and I managed the student newspaper, the vice chancellor for academic support and student life, Randy Hyman, was demoted to an assistant professor in the education department. When the news surfaced, I was in the middle of finishing two stories for that week's paper and decided to assign the story to a staff reporter.

The reporter came back from professor Hyman's office with an empty notebook, saying Hyman had no comment. If only she knew that a person who refuses to comment is the person with the most to say.

It reminded me of an obituary I was assigned during my short internship at the Tribune. I was having trouble finding someone local to comment on a man's death. I went to a senior editor and asked him for tips on locating sources. He showed me a database I could use and said, "If you don't find a source in an hour, you're fired."

I knew that approach was unnecessary as the editor of a weekly student newspaper, so I told the staff reporter she would have better luck next time and decided to take a crack at the story myself.

I walked to professor Hyman's office and sat down.

"A vice chancellor gets demoted to assistant professor," I said. "I have to ask you about that."

Hyman thanked me for coming to his office to talk face to face. He said he denied comment to the Tribune because they didn't take the time to visit him in person. Then he pointed to a coffee mug on his desk. Printed on it was a Robert Kennedy quote: "Each time a man stands for an ideal, he sends a tiny ripple of hope."

I included that gesture in my copy and hit Apple-S on my keyboard, the shortcut for saving a document.

The next week I wrote a follow-up story on the same issue. The Duluth News Tribune, admitting defeat, printed it inside the fold, spelling my name wrong in the byline.

"Maybe some day you will prove us wrong."

That comment no longer bothered me.

The bottle of port wine was running low as Joe and I sat in meditation. A Dylan and the Dead vinyl spun between songs, and the smoke began to clear in the apartment.

I told Joe that I shared with my college advisor a poem I wrote about an abused dog when I was in high school. Intrigued by the subject, my advisor enlightened me on the plight of animals in Alabama. He explained that his wife, Kim Gentry, lives there and is active with Alabama Voters for Responsible Animal Legislation (AVRAL), a political action committee lobbying for stricter laws against animal cruelty. Kim is also a singer and songwriter and donates sales profit to animal welfare groups.

My advisor put me in contact with Kim because AVRAL was looking for journalists to cover their story.

"Want to film a documentary?" I asked Joe.

"I fucking hate dogs," he said. "But I can play documentary filmmaker."

Joe pulled out a large pad of drawing paper—what he called "idea paper"— and sketched out a budget. We would need $4,000: Food, gas and lodging. The necessities.

The answer came to me. I could fulfill my love for storytelling and Joe his eagerness to travel the country in attempts to "kill all irrational fear." Together we could tell stories that needed telling. Unshackled journalism. No editor to answer to. No ratings. No cubicle. No bullshit.

Recalling what I learned about the three branches of government and the fourth estate that was necessary in keeping a system of checks and balances, I decided I didn't want to fall under any of those classifications. So Joe and I decided we would try living under a set of new guidelines. Much like Dr. Hunter Thompson's gonzo mentality, we would become the fifth estate—outliers—living and breathing the story we would one day have the wherewithal to tell.

We emailed our budget to Kim, who found an anonymous donor to sponsor our trip. The next week, we were packing our gear and heading south.

SADIE

IMAGINE A HIPPIE. ANY HIPPIE. THAT'S JOE. He has five years of hair growth matted into dreadlocks; wears a thick, colorful, poncho-like sweater; and keeps a baggy of weed in his pocket. He's carefree and speaks simply.

"Well we're going down to Alabama," Joe said. "We're going to film a documentary ... that's about as much as I know."

Before leaving Duluth, we decided to interview each other in the lobby of my apartment complex. I wanted Joe to say more and give context to what we were doing and why we were doing it. But the truth was, we had no clue what we were doing. We had no plan and no schedule, so we cut the interviews short and took off in Joe's red sedan.

Joe took the steering wheel for the first leg of the trip. He turned on a live recording of a Wide Spread Panic show and talked about the atmosphere of music festivals where everyone is drunk, drugged, and happy ... hippie shit that I wasn't very interested in but occupied the majority of Joe's daydreaming. I watched him drum his fingers on the steering wheel and spin his head from side to side so that his dreadlocks floated freely to the beat of the music.

Dirty snow banks skirted the side of the interstate, shrinking in size as we pushed beyond the boreal north woods and further south.

I watched the scenery cruise by and floated off into a daydream of my own. I thought about the poem I wrote and shared with my college advisor. The card that started the game. The reason we were on the road to Alabama.

Sadie *(Fort Smith Chocolate Lab)*

You can't please a man that finds no pleasure.
Sadie you taught me this.

Maybe that is why you were so playful,
Retrieving twigs, rocks, love,
Anything we threw.
Because once a year we filled a void,
One that needed filling,
More than he needed redemption.
And Sadie we were glad to fill it,
Easy a task it was.

When the heart is full, the mind has no worry.
Sadie you taught me this.

Maybe that is why you slept on my steps,
Through the rain and lightening,
With no distress or anguish.
Because once a year you were cared for,
You did not see it necessary to waste
A single bit of that time,
Come rain, come shine, come anything,
You soaked us up,
And Sadie I am glad you did.

Love ebbs like Montana heat, no matter the circumstance.
Sadie you taught me this.

Maybe because as the Suburban
Rolled away with my face framed in the back window,
You sat still but aware.
Because you understand life,
Its ins and outs,

Its imperfections that project on our senses
No matter how obscure they may be

When times seem unfair, it's best to be content.
Sadie you taught me this,
But if I were to have returned once more,
I would have taken you away,
Because Sadie I was not content.

When I was young, my father and I were invited to fly fish the Bighorn River in Montana with my father's coworker and his son, Paul. We stayed in a trailer home in Fort Smith, a fishing town just outside of Billings.

It was there that I learned the art of angling: double hauling, dry flies, nymphs, indicators, nail knots, blood knots, mending, drifting, waiting ... patience. I also learned not to drink water straight from the river after our guide contracted giardia, the parasite that gave him terrible diarrhea.

After a day on the river, Paul and I would play games outside the trailer home while our fathers fixed something to eat. Sadie, a chocolate Labrador, always wandered over to play with us. We didn't have a ball, so we threw the roundest rock we could find for Sadie to fetch. She trotted back to us proudly, rarely with the same rock.

One night we were hit by a thunderstorm and forced to hunker down inside. Sadie sat outside our door whimpering, and I asked my father why she refused to go home. He explained to me that home, to Sadie, meant something different. Her owner, my father said, likely abused Sadie. I wanted to let Sadie inside to stay with us, but my father told me that even though she is abused at home, it would be disrespectful to take her.

Sadie slept outside our door that night. Years later, I wrote a poem in her name.

Joe was still drumming his fingers on the steering wheel as I emerged from my daydream. The snow banks along the interstate were reduced to small piles of dirt and road salt.

I craved nature: the Bighorn River or the Boundary Waters Canoe Area Wilderness; the sunset painted on a Brown trout or the lapping of water against a canoe … something clean and simple.

I looked out the window and wondered how simple our trip to Alabama would be.

"We're going to film a documentary." I recalled what Joe said before we left.

Would it be so simple?

I closed my eyes and before long, Joe steered us off the interstate to a hotel where we loaded our footage, drank a few beers and passed out.

ALABAMA THE BEAUTIFUL

WELCOME TO ALABAMA THE BEAUTIFUL.

The sign welcoming visitors to Alabama is almost tragic. The beauty, we would learn, is difficult to find.

We met Kim and her animal rescue friend, Monnie Franziska, for brunch and Bloody Marys in Tuscaloosa. It was the first contact we made with animal rescuers, which provoked the first question: "What is an animal rescuer?"

"Rescuers are a very diverse group of people," Monnie said. "They don't all think alike."

"It's gray, like everything else," Kim added.

A rescuer can be anyone: someone who saves a stray dog, someone who lobbies for stricter animal cruelty legislation, someone with official authority to investigate animal cruelty, or someone who adopts an animal from a shelter.

Kim dodged four lanes of traffic to rescue a dog walking along interstate 65: Kim is a rescuer. Monnie rescued a stray dog that was a victim of a devastating tornado that swept across Alabama in 2012: Monnie is a rescuer.

I left Sadie in Fort Smith with her abusive owner and no one to throw rocks for her. What did that make me?

The salt from my burger and fries had me sucking down water so the waitress stopped to refill my glass. Monnie ordered a second drink and Kim dipped off to use the restroom.

We finished our food and began talking about the culture of animal cruelty in Alabama and across the Southeastern United States.

"Dog fighting is considered a culture here, too. People will say that 'this is something we've been doing for centuries, how dare you tell me I can't do something like that.' But I think what you have to remember about things that are part of a cultural norm is that it doesn't necessarily mean they are right," Monnie sounded like she was giving a Ted Talk. "So for example, for a very long time slavery was a cultural norm ... in some countries, young girls end up having their clitorises cut off because it's a cultural norm. Well, just because that is part of the culture, doesn't necessarily mean that is a humane or decent act. So I think we have to be careful when we say, 'It's part of their culture, we have to be respectful of it.' I think you have to be respectful of the culture but you don't have to necessarily like the acts that are being engaged in that culture."

Joe and I were less concerned with what was considered a cultural norm and more concerned with finding a dog fight to record on camera. Something juicy.

Kim and Monnie wanted to introduce us to rescuers with good track records willing to speak and help introduce us to issues like dog fighting.

They told us about Bonnie Miller, who is appointed by Greene County as an animal cruelty investigator, an unpaid position.

"Basically she just does it gratis," Monnie explained.

"Does she wear a bullet proof vest or something like that?" Joe asked.

"Well I'll let Bonnie tell you, but Bonnie packs pretty good ... yeah she packs," Monnie said, referring to carrying weapons. "And apparently a lot of rescuers pack."

We were eager to meet Bonnie, but we were told to contact the Greene County Humane Society President, Scott Stone, first. He would be able to introduce us to Bonnie in a nonthreatening way.

We finished our drinks, paid our bill and wrote down Scott's number.

Scott was unable to meet with us until the next day, so we had time to burn and decided to check in to our hotel on the University of Alabama campus.

"Y'all watching the game tonight?" the bartender in the hotel lobby nodded toward the television on the wall.

"What game?" I asked.

The bartender laughed, interpreting my ignorance as a joke. Apparently, the Alabama Crimson Tide was playing for the national championship that night in New Orleans, which seemed to be the reason why the campus was dry of people.

Roll Tide, Paul "Bear" Bryant, Eddie Lacy, C.J. Mosley ... things I should have known before visiting the University of Alabama. Stupid me.

We sat in the lobby arguing the importance of sports. Joe made a valid point, saying that if Alabama allocated an equal amount of money to animal welfare as it did to football, there wouldn't be a need for us to film a documentary.

It got me thinking about my own upbringing in Minnesota, where I lived and breathed the sport of hockey.

It seemed like the only thing that mattered in sports was size: My high school hockey coach told me I would have to gain 50 pounds and grow a foot over the summer to prepare for a higher caliber of hockey.

Coach Hommerding was a big guy. He grabbed my arm like it was a hockey stick, squeezed it and gave me a hearty laugh.

"Keep up the work, Davey," he patted me on the back and lumbered back down the hallway to the high school locker room where he discussed hockey systems to players twice my size. He had an intimidating stillness about him, like a giant, immovable boulder. Watching him blow the whistle for the varsity team gave me chills. He was impressed with my speed and agility but apparently concerned that none of that would matter if I didn't grow taller, or at least put on some muscle.

He was probably right. I watched my teammates grow bigger and stronger. They talked about their dicks and pubic hair so much that it made me nervous to shower after practice. They snapped towels at each other, peed on each other and compared dicks with each other. There were only a few of us who refused to shower with the team, something we became known for.

During games I shied away from physical play. Anyone who refused to "grind it out" in the corners was immediately labeled a "pussy." That year ... I was both a kid who showered at home and a pussy.

I felt furious for not being able to fix myself overnight. I tried proving myself to my teammates by boxing in the locker room. Locker boxing, we called it. Everyone would move their hockey bags to the middle of the room, forming a big circle. Two players would then put on their helmets and gloves and duke it out in the middle. I entered those fights knowing I would lose, but hoping to re-establish my reputation. Certain things mattered, certain things didn't.

But things changed when I was 14 and attended a hockey camp in the spring. Players from all over Central Minnesota signed up to learn how to shoot harder and skate faster. Coaches and instructors hooked us up to giant bungee cords and had us pull behind another player as we skated. My endurance and speed was impressive, and one of the coaches started calling me Rafalski, referring to the small, yet speedy defenseman who played for the Detroit Red Wings. I was no longer being recognized as a kid who refused to shower with the team or shy away from physical play. I was no longer a pussy. I was a hockey player.

I remember sitting in the locker room before camp. Another player wanted to locker box but nobody wanted to fight him. He was big. He kept going on about how he could "kick anyone's ass." Normally I would sit back unless someone volunteered me to fight, but I was feeling strangely confident.

"I'll fight you!" Those words made me feel good and fed me with adrenaline.

"You're too small, I don't want to hurt you too bad," Big Kid said as he turned and scanned the room for a more worthy opponent.

I was raging inside. This kid had nothing to prove. He spent most of his time talking big in the locker room, knowing nobody was stupid enough to confront him. I just spent the year being called a pussy and pointed out as a shrimp. I was slowly gaining respect and saw this fight as a way to earn it fast. I had something to fight for, he didn't.

"Just put on your helmet," I said as I snapped my cage shut.

He was taken off guard, but he couldn't back out of a fight when he was looking for one in the first place. Besides, nobody else wanted to fight him.

In past locker boxing bouts, I waited for my opponent to hit me first. I was always on the defensive, and after the first punch, I could never reverse the momentum. That wasn't going to happen this time.

I stepped in fast and landed an uppercut. I had never seen anyone lead with that technique, but I knew I wanted to try it. It worked. Big Kid stumbled back and I moved in again, punching him repeatedly. He was now bent over and leaning against the locker room bench, turned away from me. I hit him once more in the back of the head and it was over. He put up his hands to surrender. I won.

"You're just too fast," he said as he repositioned his helmet. He was complimenting me to maintain his status as a tough guy. He wanted people to know I was good and that he didn't lose to a pussy, but to someone worthy of fighting, someone who wasn't afraid to "grind it out" in the corners.

It took all day to come down from the adrenaline of that fight. I had experienced adrenaline before, but it was usually in relation to fear. This time, it was rooted in confidence and assurance of self-worth; the things that hockey taught me.

Rafalski, I thought. Now that was something I could get used to.

Sitting in the hotel lobby, nostalgia swept over me. Joe and I sipped our drinks and stared at the pre-game show.

The tradition of hockey in Minnesota, I imagined, was similar to the tradition of football in Alabama.

The next day, we met with Scott at Church's Fried Chicken in Eutaw, Alabama. Before our trip, Kim mentioned Eutaw as a place we should visit. I remember looking at a map, realizing how far apart Alabama and Utah were. It took some time to realize that Eutaw was a city in Alabama—same sound as the state of Utah, but different spelling.

We sat with Scott at a greasy table. Breaking bread. Making acquaintances. We were the only customers in the restaurant. Scott told us about his childhood growing up in Meridian, Mississippi; his career with the IBM Corporation in Atlanta, Georgia; his subsequent move to Eutaw to run a bed and breakfast out of an old antebellum home; and his new vacation home in Destin, Florida, where he retired with his wife.

I wiped my brow and tried to stomach the grease-soaked burger and fries as Scott recited the history of Eutaw in his southern drawl. The whole time he spoke, I kept thinking how much he resembled former President George W. Bush in voice, stature and mannerisms. Spitting image.

"The county was named after a revolutionary hero General Nathan Greene," Scott said.

Greene County is older than the state itself and part of the Black Belt, a region of Alabama known for its fertile soil. Early pioneers set up a network of cotton plantations across Southeastern Alabama, making it one of the wealthiest and most politically powerful regions in the United States.

Scott led us out of Church's Fried Chicken and walked us through town, pointing out historical buildings and catching us up on more history.

The dollar per gallon sign at an old gas station was stuck at $1.93. There was an H&R Block, furniture store, pizza joint, grocery store and auto repair shop. Every thirty minutes, a giant logging truck rolled through, making it hard to hear what Scott was saying. The population was less than 3,000 and 80 percent black. Everyone knew everyone, and everyone gave us a questioning eye.

"Hey! What are y'all doing?" a black man yelled from his porch.

"We're enjoying the nice day," Scott smiled. Then he turned toward Joe and I, clearly annoyed by the man's questioning. He scoffed and asked us why it was any of his business what we were doing. Scott explained how three white men walking through Eutaw was enough to raise brows. I felt like I had stepped back in time to the Jim Crow South. Signs of residual segregation were obvious in Greene County. When Scott stopped to talk with a black man who was working out of a garage, he made a point of letting us know he has a black friend, like it was some sort of oddity for people in the south to bridge racial boundaries.

As we walked out from the center of town and into the surrounding neighborhoods, we came across two female mutts hobbling along the road. Their coats were matted and wet from the rain. I shot video as they limped away alongside an old school bus. The lighting was soft and perfect.

Meanwhile, 260 miles away, Crimson Tide football fans celebrated their team's third national championship in four years, erupting in cheer and taking to Bourbon Street in droves.

I looked down the wet road. The two mutts stopped and looked back at me. To them, I was an intruder, a predator. If I were to return to Fort Smith, maybe Sadie would see me the same way.

I felt nauseated.

It was our first sighting of animal despair and I thought I would be sad, but instead, I was angry. Maybe Joe was right. Maybe the priorities in the South were fucked.

Roll Tide, Paul "Bear" Bryant, Eddie Lacy, C.J. Mosley, national championships, bumper stickers, window flags, touchdowns, victories, clamoring crowds, pride, and unity ...

Alabama the Beautiful, I thought, wincing at the irony.

"THIS IS ONE THAT WILL REALLY BLOW YOUR DRESS UP"

As promised, Scott drove us along several miles of winding county road to Bonnie's house, which is situated on a hill overlooking a small pond.

Remembering what Kim and Monnie said about Bonnie packing heat and being a little bit crazy, I was nervous. As I watched the countryside roll by, I tried to picture her: scraggly, smelling of cat urine and speaking sporadically.

When we drove up Bonnie's gravel driveway, several yard dogs greeted us. A beefy Rottweiler and a three-legged mutt wearing colorful handkerchiefs around their collars stood out to me.

Scott honked the car horn and Bonnie stepped out from the house. She wasn't how I imagined her. She looked normal. She wore blue jeans and a salmon-colored hoodie. Her hair was light brown with streaks of blond, dried from the sun. She smiled and waved to us as we stepped out of the car.

We made introductions and thanked Bonnie for agreeing to be featured in our documentary. She introduced us to her husband, Tim, who was spreading cedar chips around dog kennels in the backyard. We tried to start a conversation, but the dogs were making too much noise and Bonnie decided to feed them so they would quiet down.

We shot video of Bonnie and Tim tending to their nightly routine. Bonnie fed and watered the 40 rescue dogs as Tim picked up poop from their kennels and runs. We watched them and they watched us, like dogs sniffing each other's butts for the first time, cautiously excited.

Bonnie disappeared into the house and came out with an accordion-style binder filled with documents and pictures from cases of animal cruelty she had investigated. She sat down on the steps and thumbed through files.

"Oh this is one that will really blow your dress up," Bonnie stood and held a picture out in front of us. "Check this out, you want to see some crap?"

The picture showed a pit bull whose ears had been cut off by its owner to make the dog look fierce. A woman's hand was framed in the forefront, pinning what was left of the dog's ears together with a clothespin so they could stick upright.

Fuck, I thought, and looked up at Bonnie who was already sizing up my reaction.

"That's customary around here with pit fighters. They cut their dog's ears off at home with pocket knives, scissors ..." Bonnie paused, tucked her chin down and stared at me above the rims of her glasses, checking to see if the story was sinking in. "Man, it's customary 'round here," her voice rose an octave.

My eyes were pulled wide in awe, partly with disgust over the image and partly out of fear of Bonnie. I didn't know what to say or how to react. I had no reference of severe animal cruelty, so I simply stood there dumbly, slack-jawed and naive.

Bonnie flipped through more pictures of bloodied animals. There were so many she had trouble remembering the corresponding cruelty case for each one. She stopped flipping whenever a picture caught her eye and would start telling the story behind an image until she saw another one she remembered, at which point she would move on to a new story. Bonnie admitted to having attention deficit disorder.

"Her master is a scumbag of all scumbags," Bonnie turned so Joe could see the picture. "They did a pit bust ... the sheriff called me out at 6 o'clock one morning and I hadn't had my coffee so it was hard for me to go but anyway ... I went because I always wanted this guy. I had him in court four times and this was his fifth."

Bonnie explained to us the difficulty in pinning down dog fighters.

"You have to catch them in the act for it to be a felony." She paused again and stared at us and said, without actually saying anything, that catching a pit fighter in the act is damn near impossible.

I could sense Bonnie's frustration as she scanned over more photos. Dozens of cases flashed in her memory, dredging up old emotion.

It started to rain and Bonnie told Joe to watch out for his camera so we retreated underneath the breezeway. Scott had been inside using the restroom and came out to meet us. He started talking about a magazine and the still imagery in it and asked us if still images could be used in our film. Bonnie never got to finish her story, but we got the idea: cruelty is a part of the culture in Greene County. It's customary.

We made plans to join Scott and Bonnie at the Greene County Humane Society meeting the next day. Then we drove back to our hotel in Tuscaloosa.

As I loaded footage from the day, I started getting anxious knowing we had been in Alabama for six days and only logged one interview and some scenic footage. Everything seemed to be progressing slowly. As Scott put it, we would need to meet people first and interview them later. Share a beer and get to know the source before unpacking the camera gear. I was attracted to the idea of doing journalism differently, but simply didn't have the time. My ten days off from a broadcast news job in Minnesota were almost up and we were nowhere near close enough to gathering enough material for a documentary.

=

TORNADO HUNTERS

WE HAD TIME TO KILL BEFORE THE HUMANE SOCIETY MEETING and decided to go for a drive. The plan was to find a dogfight. We would pull up to a whole-in-the-wall bar and Joe would smoke a joint with some thugs who would then invite us to their dogfight. A simple plan stripped of all common sense.

As we rounded a wide curve on Martin Luther King Boulevard, I saw a dead dog on the side of the road. Joe pulled a U-turn and we drove back to check it out. Sure as shit, a brindle pit bull with a wire tied around its neck lay in the ditch by a stripped old tire and a green river of garbage.

We filmed the carnage in every way imaginable: wide shots, shots of the wire, close-ups of the dog's crusty and lifeless eyes. As photojournalists, we thought we hit the jackpot, the image that would tell the entire story of abuse and abandonment in Alabama ... a nameless dog, dead and forgotten. Pure tragedy. Life Magazine shit.

When we were done filming, we sat in the car in silence, coming down from the adrenaline. I started thinking about the dog's life before it ended up dead on the side of the road. Was it abused? Was it a fighting dog? Did it break free from its chain?

I told Joe to call animal control and report the incident and I would film the interaction, which felt like staged journalism, but I wanted answers. Maybe they would have a better idea of where the dog came from and if Bonnie was right about the culture of cruelty being customary in Alabama.

"Animal control, how may I help you?" the dispatcher asked.

"Yeah I just ran across a dead dog along the side of the road about a quarter mile out of town down Martin Luther King Boulevard." Joe held the phone out so I could better hear the conversation.

"Ok, we'll see if they can find it," the line crackled and Joe hung up.

Twenty minutes later, two animal control officers—one old and one young—jumped out of their truck to greet us.

We told them we were in town filming wreckage from the tornado when we spotted a dead dog and decided to call it in. Then we bullshitted for a while.

"Y'all in school here or y'all just here filming?" the older of the two officers asked as he shook open a black garbage bag, peaking out the meter on our audio recorder.

"We're just getting some warm air, man. We're from Minnesota, so ..." Joe said as we followed the officers to where the dog lay in the ditch.

"This is actually in the county, but we come through here sometimes and we see something like this and try to get it off the road," the younger officer said.

The older officer then wrapped the dog up in the garbage bag, folding its limbs in, flipping the bag inside out, and pulling up on the edges so the dog could fall to the bottom of the bag like a giant ham. Then he looked up at us, smiling.

"Do y'all want it ... to carry it home for a souvenir?" he asked.

We laughed nervously.

"Well, do y'all know where to go to see all the storm damage?" the older officer asked, trying to be helpful.

"Yeah," I lied, almost forgetting they didn't know we were filming a documentary on animal abuse, not the tornado damage.

"So how often do you guys pick up dead dogs on the side of the road?" I changed the topic.

"All the time," the older officer said, hauling the animal back toward the truck. "We pick up more dead than we do live. The dead won't bite you, remember that."

The younger officer said on average they pick up five or six dead dogs per day, which amounts to at least 100 a month, far exceeding what I had expected.

We maintained our intentions of filming tornado damage and accepted parting advice from the officers. They told us to check out Alberta City, a neighborhood in northeastern Tuscaloosa where the tornado hit hard.

"We will," I said, then watched the officers drive back down Martin Luther King Boulevard with the dead dog lumped on the tailgate.

We got back in the car and made it a half mile down the road when I spotted two stray dogs that had been eating from a dead deer carcass. We followed them to a torn up, blue storage container—their home—and shot video as they hobbled away from us.

It was heartbreaking to see domesticated animals that no longer showed trust toward human beings. Someone, at some point, failed them miserably.

The storage container had been bent from the tornado in a way that made one end hover above the ground like a cantilever. Both dogs had retreated to the back of the container. I zoomed in with my camera lens, trying to capture one last shot, when the dogs walked back out from the container and stood together on the edge of the cantilevered opening. I don't know if they were asking to be rescued, but at that moment, they were beautiful. I wanted to help them but didn't know how, so I turned my camera off and walked back to the car, feeling my heart sink further into my chest, followed by an onslaught of confusion and culture shock.

As we drove back toward Eutaw to meet Bonnie and Scott for the Greene County Humane Society Meeting, I thought about what it meant to be a journalist: unbiased and fair, factual and detailed, relentless and delicate. I thought about what my journalism professor would say when I told him I lied to animal control officers about being a tornado hunter. I could see his reaction, his silence and raised eyebrows. He would ask me how I planned on handling that footage in the documentary. He would warn me that I could be sued. I started feeling like I was failing and that maybe the idea of a documentary didn't make sense. Maybe I wasn't ready for it.

I looked out the window as we passed exits leading to rural county roads where more dead animals peppered the ditches. Somewhere, not far off the interstate, someone was failing another dog miserably, forcing it to fight to the death. Someone was shooting up heroine and someone was getting paid to spill blood. Someone was tossing a dead animal in the bed of their truck, driving a fair distance from the fighting ring, and dumping it off on the side of the road for animal control officers to stumble upon. Five to six per day and at least 100 per month. Somewhere out there, someone wasn't playing by the rules, so why the fuck should I?

I'll be a tornado hunter if I have to, I thought.

ALL GUSSIED UP

IT WAS GOOD TO SEE BONNIE AGAIN, especially after deciding I would no longer give a fuck about law and ethics. I felt like one of her people, driven by a greater cause. We stood outside in the church parking lot, waiting for Joe to finish a cigarette before going inside for the humane society meeting.

We had been promised anonymous donors would cover our hotel costs, which was necessary considering I had 400 dollars in my account and Joe's credit cards were all maxed out from outdoor gear purchases. We had been staying at the Capstone Hotel in Tuscaloosa for four nights and were concerned we would be stuck unable to pay our bill. When we shared the information with Bonnie, her hackles went up and said she would make a phone call. We told her not to worry about it, but when Bonnie sets her mind to something, there is no stopping her.

Joe and I set up our cameras and placed a circular microphone in the center of the table before the humane society meeting began. I was expecting a fair few people, but the meeting only included Bonnie, Scott, Monnie, and a lady whose name I can't remember but reminded me of one of those crazy cat ladies you see in the movies.

Scott started the meeting by sharing a story about a litter of puppies that got "mashed"—whatever that meant. He stressed the need for a proper animal shelter in Greene County so stray dogs would have a suitable place to be vetted and adopted out, and so puppies would no longer end up getting "mashed."

The group threw around ideas, discussing the issue of ignorance in the county that extended its slimy tentacles within local government. Monnie stressed the importance of education and planting the seed early in youth so that the culture of cruelty will slowly die off with a generation. For the most part, everyone seemed more interested in philosophizing for our cameras than discussing realistic, smaller-scale solutions.

Then Bonnie cut in and explained that a shelter sounds "fine and dandy," but wouldn't necessarily solve the problem, the root of which would take decades to fix. She shared a story about a shelter in a neighboring county where she heard reports of the director abusing the animals for fun.

"He's kin to everybody in the county, he's kin to the commissioner ... his uncle's a judge," Bonnie leaned in over the table to emphasize the problem of the good old boys club restricting action in the area.

Bonnie had a picture of a dog that was housed at the shelter. There was a deer carcass—what the shelter fed the dogs—and blood in the picture. The blood, however, was not deer blood, rather blood from a recent injury incurred by the dog while in the shelter.

"So I pretended like I was a single lady. I went down there kinda somewhat gussied up because I had heard he liked ladies." Bonnie's plan was to flirt with the shelter director in hopes he would take a liking to her and hand over the abused dog.

"He had loaded all the rest of the dogs on my vehicle, but this one dog I couldn't get from him and I just really kept praying about it. I said 'Lord, look. I cannot leave this dog here in that condition. You gotta give me something, you gotta help me here.' So I finally crawled in my vehicle and he starts kind of flirting around. Well, I start flirting back 'cause I'm ready to get this dog out and I thought whatever it takes, this dog is coming with me today. So he says, 'Would you consider dating a black guy?' and I said, 'Well, I might,' and kinda giggling, flirting."

Bonnie stopped to explain to the group that she had no trouble with blacks and whites dating; she just wanted to get the dog out.

"I'm not saying I have a racial issue here, don't get me wrong. What I'm saying is I'm married and undercover here pretending to be a single lady.

"He kept wanting my phone number and finally I said, 'I tell you what, you get me the dog, and I'll give you my phone number.' So finally, he goes and gets the dog," Bonnie leaned in again, patted Monnie on the arm, and laughed.

"And I assume you gave him a false phone number?" Scott asked.

"No ... no, no, no, I didn't, I gave him my real cell number. I don't give a crap. So anyway, he called me that night."

We stopped by a liquor store to pick up two six packs of Abita, beer native to the region. Feeling somewhat moved by the humanitarian efforts of Bonnie, I gave a homeless man my spare change. Then we drove back to the hotel to make plans for the next day.

I opened my reporter's notebook and glanced at a list of names and numbers we had been given.

Bobbi Taylor, a 78-year-old woman who had rescued more than 10,000 animals in her lifetime, stood out to me, so I called her. We chatted briefly on the phone and made plans to meet.

When we woke up the next day, our hotel bill had been paid. I thought about Bonnie and smiled.

By lipstick or by gun, I thought. *Nothing can stop that lady.*

BOBBI TAYLOR

Driving up Highway 43 toward Moulton, Alabama to meet Bobbi was a real trip. Just as we reached the outskirts of Tuscaloosa, we began spotting dead dogs everywhere. We filmed them all, each time with slightly less surprise, expecting to see a dead dog every 15 miles. I had seen enough and feared I was becoming immune to the tragedy ... a part of the problem.

When it was Joe's turn to drive I caught up on text messages from my girlfriend back home. She was nervous about me meeting a bunch of girls in Alabama. I laughed at the irony as we stopped to film another dead dog.

It's been quite the party down here, I thought, turning my head from a shaggy, black dog half submerged in a puddle of water, preventing myself from throwing up in the ditch.

We cut east and drove through William B. Bankhead National Forest, which was beautiful: tall trees and thick forests hugged tightly to the rolling blacktop. We were in awe of the exposed tree roots, tangling across the forest floor, and decided at that moment to name our documentary, "Roots of Rescue."

Bobbi's driveway was a muddy mess and I almost lost a sandal as we walked up to her backdoor with our camera gear. The sun was already below the horizon and I couldn't see the kennels in her yard, but I knew they were there because when we rapped on Bobbi's back door, a fury of barking ensued.

Bobbi was wearing a bright red sweater and a tan hat that hid her hair, making her look like a cancer patient. I wondered if maybe she was. She certainly was old enough for it to be a likely possibility.

She led us through her kitchen, which was full of occupied dog kennels, and into her living room where her friend, Connie Ray Livingston, greeted us. Connie Ray wanted to speak on camera about an animal cruelty incident in his neighborhood.

We decided to interview Connie Ray first so Bobbi could familiarize herself with the process and feel more at ease with the cameras and lights.

Connie Ray told us a story about his neighbor, Carl, whose dog had been hung on Christmas day from a loft in his barn. Carl had cut the dog down just before calling Connie Ray, who told him to hang the dog back up and call the police. Carl told the investigator his neighbors might have done it, because Carl had called the police on them for dealing drugs in the past.

The story included a lot of hearsay: Carl's neighbors doing drugs in his barn, Carl's wife firing a shotgun at them, the neighbors then accusing Carl of having sex with his dog on a trampoline. The story spun out of control quickly, so Joe and I cut the interview short because it was too fucked up to make any sense of. And in the end, nothing was done about the incident, so there were no official documents to work from. But we got the idea: A feud between neighbors resulted in the death of an innocent gray and white bulldog.

We thanked Connie Ray for his time then focused our attention on Bobbi. I asked her about her history with animal rescue.

"When I was very young I witnessed a neighbor beating two mules to death that could not pull an overloaded wagon out of a mud hole, and it affected me so much that I vowed to God that I would spend my life helping animals, and I've done my very best to do that.

"The important thing for America to realize is that I don't care how many laws you pass, it's to no avail if the law enforcement doesn't enforce those laws and make it a felony to abuse animals the way they are being abused, mostly in the south." Bobbi reminded me of Bonnie, sharp and to the point. Very humble.

The night before our interview with Bobbi, we were watching the local news from our hotel when reports of animal cruelty in Athens, Alabama came on. The story was about a man, Mr. Tunstill, who shot and killed his neighbor's six-month-old black lab for barking at his chickens. The man then burned the dog in a pile of debris in his backyard in attempts to cover up the dog's death.

"Mr. Tunstill has a right to protect his property and chickens, but he probably didn't use good judgment disposing of the animal," Limestone County Sheriff Mike Blakely told reporters. He went on to say that it's possible that both parties could be arrested: Mr. Tunstill for not disposing of the dog "properly," and the dog owner for not keeping better track of the animal.

"Our sheriff's office, like in most rural areas, spends a good portion of our time dealing with neighbors who don't get along," Blakely told the Huntsville Times. "Many people want the government to solve all the problems, but people have got to learn to be good neighbors."

Joe gave me another one of those looks, the kind that said—without saying—*is this real life? Modern life? Happening right now? In 21st century?*

If my neighbor shot and killed my dog and then proceeded to burn it in a pile of brush, I would expect my government to consider the issue to be more than a customary dispute between neighbors. In fact, Alabama law defines animal cruelty as a felony, but if you read the exemptions to the law, it's evident that the law is essentially mute.

Exemption three states: "Any person who kills a dog or cat found outside of the owned or rented property of the owner or custodian of the dog or cat when the dog or cat threatens immediate physical injury or is causing physical injury to any person, animal, bird, or silvicultural or agricultural industry."

As Bobbi put it, "The secret to all of this ... it's people." People like Mr. Tunstill who kill without reason, and people like Sheriff Blakely who write off animal cruelty as a dispute between neighbors. Ignorance breeds ignorance.

"If you could say something to these people, what would you tell them?" I asked.

Bobbi laughed and told us we probably don't want to know. Then, without hesitation, she told us anyway.

"I hope the same thing happens to them, only tenfold. I hope they suffer before they die.

"But you know what? Bad karma will get them. They'll end up being repaid," she said with a nod of certainty.

On that note, we ended the interview and made plans to meet up the next morning so Bobbi could show us around her property. We rented a room at the cheapest motel in Moulton where the manager behind the check-in counter tried selling us used mattresses even after we told him we were just visiting from Minnesota.

We couldn't escape the stupidity.

When we visited Bobbi in 2012, there was an operating shelter in her county: The Animal House Zoological Society—home to rescued, exotic animals—was owned and operated by Carolyn Atchison. Her land and established facility meant the county didn't have to build a shelter, a win-win of sorts. The county paid her a $70,000 salary plus a truck, gas and cellphone.

"It's about 15 miles out of town, it's behind closed gates, and if she doesn't want you on the property, she won't let you on the property." Bobbi explained that the Animal House is on Carolyn's private land, making it difficult for people like Bobbi to rescue animals there.

"Most of the people bring me their dogs, they don't want to take them to the local animal shelter because they know they're going to be killed and in their opinion it's a horrible place. The 28 that I took yesterday were all owner-surrendered to me," Bobbi said.

The month we visited, Bobbi had rescued 86 dogs, which she sent to Bideawee, an animal welfare organization on the East side of Long Island, New York, and the Animal Rescue Fund in New York. I thought it was funny that she sent her dogs to New York, where dog lovers would pay hundreds of dollars for dogs that people in the south shot at from their front porches or burned in their backyards, just before shouting *Roll Tide*. The dichotomy made me smile, imagining a dog that was once pissed on, now fluffed and pampered in the Hamptons. Bobbie said she didn't care if someone got $1,000 for a dog, as long as it found a good home.

"How many animals have you saved?" I asked.

"I stopped counting at 12,000. I have six boxes of records and pictures dating back to 1940." I zoomed in on Bobbi's face with my camera lens as she said, "12,000," a cinematography trick I had picked up that helped put greater emphasis on what the subject was saying, something that required foresight and good timing. I realized later that it wasn't necessary, because rescuing over 12,000 animals was shocking enough and didn't require fancy camera tricks to make the hair on people's necks stand up.

"So how does it make you feel thinking about that … 12,000 lives?" I asked.

"Very humble." Bobbi's eyes welled up. "I didn't set out to do it, it just happened, I just never quit.

"When I was six, seven, eight, nine, ten, all the way through high school I would watch the Model T's or the wagons go to town. I lived right by a little creek and I would sit on the bridge on Saturdays and watch the wagons go to town and if they threw a bundle in the creek, I knew it had kittens and puppies in it and I would run down, jump in the creek and get them out. Then when I would accumulate a lot in the barn my daddy would look at me and say, 'Bobbi Jean,' and I knew what he meant, they had to go. So I'd put them in feed sacks and cut holes in the sacks for their little heads to stick out. I'd tie the feed sacks together and throw them over my horse's shoulders and I'd go all over the countryside giving them away.

"I don't think what I've done is so extraordinary. A lot of people think it is, but the pleasure really has been mine. I've been repaid," Bobbi said.

In 2014, the mayor of Moulton proclaimed May 3 Bobbi Taylor Day in honor of the pioneer of animal rescue in Alabama. She has also raised a considerable amount of money through fundraisers with London Jewelers and Animal Planet's Jack Hanna for an animal shelter she plans to build in Lawrence County. But the repayment she was referring to was different. Sitting in her living room, which was stripped of furniture that she donated to tornado victims, it's obvious that Bobbi is in it for the right reasons. I paused before asking my next question, watching Bobbi's smile fill the room, realizing she had every intention of fulfilling her vow to save animals until the day she dies.

I called Bobbi two years after our interview. She was busy "putting a cat up." I didn't know what that meant but I realized it was life as usual for her. I imagined her shuffling through her kitchen filled with dog crates with a cat in one hand and the phone in the other.

She caught me up on the changes happening in Lawrence County.

For reasons unknown but highly speculated, the county decided to discontinue its contract with Atchison and the Animal House, and two days later, Atchison visited the Commission office and turned in her keys to county administrator Tricia Galbreath. The county then filed suit against Atchison for breaching her contract, asking for $16,153.99 back from work paid for but not performed.

Bobbi is now vying for the vacant animal control contract and getting closer to reaching her fundraising goal that will make it possible for her to build a pro-life shelter in Lawrence County.

"I'm going to put it in a trust so these stupid commissioners can't sell it," she said. "We're going to clean up this county."

She told me to keep in touch and wished me luck with writing this book. I paused again, much like I had when Bobbi first told me she has rescued more than 12,000 dogs.

"I will," I said. "Really nice talking to you again."

Then I sent Joe a text message saying it was a trip talking to Bobbi again, and that her county no longer has a shelter but that she's still working to raise money to build one.

"Shit don't slow down in Bama," Joe wrote back.

ANATOMY OF
A RESCUE

MONNIE, BONNIE, BOBBI ... it only made sense that the next rescuer we were going to meet was Robbie. My reporter's notebook was a real cluster-fuck of similar sounding names.

We drove the five hours from Moulton to Mobile, but just before we reached the city, we spotted more dead dogs on the side of the road: one with a mouthful of maggots, one near the driveway of a private residence, one in a plastic storage container and one lying ironically close to a cross in the ditch signifying a fatal traffic accident. We knelt down on the side of the interstate to film them all.

I held my breath as I panned my camera from a middle school building down to a dead dog across the street. It was hard to tell if it was the stench of rotting flesh or the juxtaposition of a dead dog near a school that was making me gag.

I let my camera roll for five more seconds, ensuring I would be able to use the video clip for a fast or slow edit, and then ran back toward the car for fresh air.

Joe was finishing a cigarette and tying a bandanna around his neck, which he pulled up over his mouth to mask the smell. Then he started walking toward the dog to get a closeup—macro shot—of maggots eating the insides of the animal. I stuffed my cheek with a handful of salty sunflower seeds and watched him do his thing.

People honked at us as they sped by, probably wondering what in the hell we were doing filming dead animals. To them, those dogs were nothing more than roadkill.

I eyed the honking drivers and spat sunflower seeds toward the ground in a *go fuck yourself* manner. Anger swept over me. I felt like everyone in Alabama was to blame, and hoped—in a knee-jerk way—that Mexico would annex the South, but as we drove into Mobile, Joe and I agreed that we had only scraped the surface of the story, one that went much deeper than a debate between right and wrong.

We called Robbie, telling her we would be at the hotel shortly, and could meet her for dinner.

Robbie used to work as the food and beverage manager at the Riverview Plaza Hotel in downtown Mobile—one of the tallest buildings on Mobile's cityscape—so she hooked us up with a suite on the top level of the building overlooking the bay.

I smelled like cigars and was covered in sunflower seed residue. The clerk in the lobby stepped out from behind the counter to shake my hand, telling me our suite was ready. I didn't know what Robbie told the man, but clearly he thought I was someone of importance … a West Coast filmmaker with a list of credentials. I smiled back and took the hotel keys before Joe gave me another one of those *how the fuck did we end up here?* looks. I gave him the same look in return as we entered the elevator where we had to use our room key to access the suite level.

On our way into Mobile, we made the mistake of eating a bag full of fast food, so I spent most of the night on the toilet with the worst diarrhea, which subsequently forced Joe to evacuate the room to smoke a joint. Cleary the universe was correcting its mistake of putting us in a top-level suite. I stripped down, put on the fluffy robe from the closet hutch, turned on the NHL Network, and waited for another bowel movement as the sun set over the bay outside our window.

Up to that point, the title 'rescuer' was quite vague and difficult to explain. Ask Bonnie or Bobbi what it means to be a rescuer and they might not be able to answer. In Mobile, however, where thousands of dogs are euthanized at animal shelters every year, rescue is simple: Pull dogs that are facing euthanasia, find them foster homes and adopt them out. There were four groups in the city using that formula at the time of our visit. Robbie was affiliated with South Bark and working on opening her own shelter, Safe Haven Animal Care Kennels, or the SHACK.

"Once the dogs come in they have seven days," Robbie said, referring to dogs that come into shelters that are at capacity. It's what rescuers call 'death row.'

Robbie is middle aged and overworked. I don't know if she is a caffeine addict but all the signs were there: She moved and spoke fast, she had a long list of things to do and was keenly aware of the clock. We followed her as she walked through the Mobile County Animal Shelter, where she gets a list of dogs that, because of their breed, are rescue only. As a rescuer, she walks through the shelter, takes photos of the dogs, posts them to Facebook, and waits for someone to agree to either adopt or foster. She knew all the dogs by name.

"She has 'til Wednesday." Robbie pointed to a brindle pit bull that was licking her fingers through the kennel gate. Then another, and another ... a whole row of animals that had less than a week to live. Robbie broke down in tears as she stopped to pet a black, mixed breed dog that had its paws up on the kennel door and was looking at Robbie with glossy, desperate eyes, like a scene out of an American Humane Society public service announcement.

"As much as we even do this ... last year the intake was 7,414 and 4,600 were euthanized.

"The people at the shelter itself, they really care. It breaks their hearts to have to euthanize so many." We cut our cameras out of respect as Robbie broke down into tears again. Then she explained to us the issue of overpopulation and a lack of education regarding spaying and neutering.

"A lot of people just don't understand. They think that the dog is still a disposable commodity in the South," she said.

Robbie said goodbye to a row of animals—possibly for the last time—before we left the shelter. In the parking lot, a man asked us if the shelter was open, because he wanted to drop off his dog. Then he gave us his business card and asked if we would film a music video for his rap group.

Following Robbie is not easy: When she jumps in her SUV, she hits the gas and doesn't stop because her time is limited. Joe and I were scrambling to keep up with her, and I left our microphone stand on the roof of the car on our way to the TLC Veterinary Hospital. I looked in the rearview mirror as the stand rolled off the roof, bounced off the trunk and was absorbed by oncoming traffic.

Robbie introduced us to the TLC veterinarian, Dr. Leonard, who works closely with rescue groups in Mobile. There was a yellow lab-mix walking around her office that had been abused and for some reason, didn't like men. So when the dog jumped up and wrapped its front legs around me, Dr. Leonard was surprised and told me I had to adopt him. I thought about it for a moment even considering my apartment back in Minnesota didn't allow pets.

Dr. Leonard is a small lady with short blonde hair, but she carries with her an air of authority. She was hesitant to go on camera, but Robbie twisted her arm, ensuring her that it's really not that bad unless you start crying. They joked for a minute and then Dr. Leonard agreed to an on-camera interview.

We framed an abused dog in the foreground of our shots so Dr. Leonard could use it as an example of what she sees.

"In the South, in general, how big is the problem?" I asked.

"Unfortunately, it's huge. I think society has become such a disposable one." Dr. Leonard looked down at the dog on the table in front of her. It couldn't have weighed more than 10 pounds and was quivering in its small frame. Someone had dumped the dog off on the side of the road, something Dr. Leonard says happens all too often.

I went for the heartstrings with my next question.

"How does it make you feel?"

"Frustrated, angry … sick." She looked back down at the quivering dog. "I don't understand how people can do this to an animal, to be honest. They're so innocent and loyal." I could tell she was beyond crying. She was fed up and maybe even desensitized. Anger and frustration were all that remained.

The yellow dog then wandered over to me and sat by my feet, where he stayed during the entire interview. I didn't know he was there until Dr. Leonard pointed it out.

I asked Dr. Leonard to give me an example of an abused animal she's had to help, and she recounted two separate incidences where dogs were dropped off with arrows stuck in them. Then she shared the story of a dog that had been shot in the rear. Laughing nervously, she paused and said there have been so many incidents that it's hard to recall the details of a single one.

"Honestly, its once a week, that's what's so frustrating about the whole thing ... and ridiculous," she added.

Before meeting Dr. Leonard, Robbie explained to us the tension between rescuers and vets. Some vets, she said, get upset with rescue groups and low-cost spay and neuter programs because they cut in on their business. Dr. Leonard, however, referred to rescuers as angels and a saving grace.

"We can only do so much as far as education where we are at. It's really the community and the people on the outside that can help," she said.

"What's the final solution?" Joe asked.

Dr. Leonard said a combination of education and more spay and neuter programs are a good start. She said the mentality also has to change, something she was more pessimistic about.

"Is it a situation that is ever going to get better? I hope so, but honestly, probably not." Her pessimism was sad, but the hardened truth is often difficult to digest.

At the end of the interview, Dr. Leonard handed me our microphone and said, "You need to take the dog home with you," gesturing toward the yellow dog that was still trailing me through the office.

I looked down at him and smiled. Knowing I couldn't take him broke my heart.

If only my apartment complex was dog friendly, I thought.

It made me think of Robbie walking through the shelter, petting animals she knows will likely be euthanized unless someone sees her posts on Facebook and decides to help. Despite her best efforts, more often than not—4,600 times a year—the dogs are put down.

I wondered how many *if only* thoughts had gone through Robbie's head. As a rescuer, she has committed herself to a constant state of heartbreak and mourning, which begs the question: Why?

It's a question Robbie and all of the rescuers we met couldn't fully answer because they didn't have time to ask it of themselves. I was beginning to pick up on the pulse of animal rescue. It's seeing something so horrific that you can't turn away. It's standing on the side of the road next to a dead dog letting the stench of rotting flesh fill your lungs. It's visiting a shelter and letting a dog that has hours to live lick your fingers through the kennel door. It's receiving a business card from a man more concerned with his rap group than the well-being of his dog. It's a million *if only* statements running through your head. It's a yellow dog that won't leave your side.

Our visit with Robbie seemed to end before it began. We chased her around town all day, fitting neatly in the window of time she set aside for animal rescue. I felt for her and hoped she would find time for a vacation or a day trip to the beach. But as long as there were dogs being slaughtered, it was clear where Robbie would be.

We drove to Gulf Shores that night to interview Sandra Nathan, a reporter and research chair for Alabama Voters for Responsible Animal Legislation (AVRAL). It's her job to research animal legislation in Alabama and compare it to states that are more progressive in law and ideology.

Her home was blocks away from the Gulf. When we pulled up we could taste salt in the air. As a writer, I was excited to meet a fellow journalist.

Sandra's voice was gravely from years of cigarette smoking, and as we would learn, many Harley Rides to Daytona. She was raw and uncut, like most of the animal activists we encountered.

She gave us both a can of Coke before we sat down for the interview. We turned the color temperature of our lights up so there would be a contrast between the warm tones on Sandra's face and the cool evening light coming in through the sunroom. As she started explaining her role in animal rescue, Joe cracked his can of Coke open, rendering the audio of her description useless. Clearly, we weren't an experienced documentary film crew from California or some place with highly regarded film schools. We were just two guys with cameras and subpar audio equipment trying to wade through the pile of cultural bullshit in Alabama.

"When you find a dog chained, or otherwise outside, the law says the owner must provide shelter. Well, shelter can be interpreted by the law enforcement. It can be a piece of board on top of a stone as far as they're concerned.

"Every county must provide a suitable animal pound. There the word is 'suitable.'" Sandra explained to us how a law could look good until certain words like 'shelter' or 'suitable' were concerned, leaving the law up for interpretation.

We recorded four interviews and were starting to realize we were listening to a broken record: Education, spay and neuter, stricter laws, and better law enforcement—the pillars of animal welfare. The tangibles of rescue—the legwork—were only a Band-Aid for a more complicated, cultural issue.

"A lot of it is blamed on ignorance. Personally I don't excuse that.

"You can rescue every one of the animals from the animal shelter today, just like the ones you saw. Before the week is out, it will be filled again." Sandra explained how stricter laws could help the people "in the trenches," but in the end, there would still be a cultural issue to address.

"We can't legislate compassion.

"We want to search for the 'why' ... the reasons," Sandra stressed. "Rescue is the only thing we can do right now."

And therein lie the problems and the need for a new plan, a network of rogue animal rescuers, a down south justice.

It was time to follow Bonnie in the field and witness the culture of cruelty first hand, and maybe uncover the 'who' and 'why' of animal abuse.

"I'M ONE LADY
OUT HERE"

"DID SOMEBODY SODOMIZE THAT DOG?" It was 9 AM when Joe asked that question. We had loaded dog crates and camera gear into Bonnie's SUV and drove no more than three miles down the road before Bonnie pulled over to inspect a dead dog, whose rear end was bloodied and injured.

Bonnie was kneeling next to the dog, lifting its head with her bare hand. A car slowed down to watch and caught Bonnie's attention.

"Man, get the hell on out of here now I'm really busy," she voiced under her breath, tracking the car as it rolled by.

Then she refocused her attention to the dog.

"I think someone shot the dog in the rear end, if you want to know my honest opinion.

"He's pit bull. He's thin. He has some old injuries up under here." Bonnie lifted the dog's leg, revealing a wound to its inner thigh. I could see the dog's bone through the wound and felt sick to my stomach.

"Most of the dogs in this county are going to have injuries of some sort. You have to understand, this is what I'm trying to tell you now," I zoomed out from the dog's injury and refocused my camera on Bonnie, anticipating a good sound bite.

"The culture in this county is pathetic. You know this dog has old injuries on the insides of its legs and God knows what happened to him. Maybe someone just shot him because they didn't want him around. But this is common. This is everywhere.

"If you guys got your shots, we'll go ahead, because this is just the beginning," Bonnie ushered us back to the vehicle so she could start some real investigating.

"Be careful, guys. Careful, careful!" Bonnie warned us about making our cameras blatantly visible as we drove through the ghetto.

We pulled off onto a dirt road in Forklund, Alabama. Bonnie drove slowly, looking for signs of dog fighting.

The first driveway we pulled into had two pit bulls tied up, both attached to large tractor chains. Bonnie got out of the SUV to check them out. One was scarred up from a pit bull fight, but the owner wasn't home so we moved on.

I lifted my camera above the dashboard as we pulled into the next driveway.

"Y'all kinda keep those cameras down," Bonnie said as she stepped out of the vehicle, telling us to stay put unless she gave us the go ahead. I felt like a soldier waiting for my orders to charge.

There was a man in the backyard that looked suspicious to Bonnie, so she walked back behind the house to talk with him.

"Hey. How you doing? Are those your pits? Are you the guy I talked to before?" She made her way around the side of the house where a row of hedges made it difficult to see what was happening.

"Have you still got that Australian Shepherd?" Bonnie berated the man with multiple questions, which confused the man and allowed Bonnie to edge into his space.

"Ma'am?" the man's head bobbed up above the hedges. I let half of my camera lens peek above the dashboard to get a shot. The frame showed the interaction in the top half and blurry dashboard in the bottom half. Joe made a comment that he liked the composition. We filmed what we could while the audio recorder we sent with Bonnie picked up the interaction.

"You had an Australian Shepherd you got from, um … from Cliff." Bonnie paused. "Are you the same guy I talked to?"

"I ain't got no dog from Cliff," the man snapped back.

Bonnie told him he was lying and that he used to have an Australian Shepherd. She was sure of it.

"I aint never fool with no Shepherd," he said.

They never made introductions. Bonnie knew who he was and he certainly knew who Bonnie was. He mulled around in the backyard while Bonnie walked over to a dog to check its collar. It took her a minute to settle the dog down. She found some injuries to its nose, which the man said came from a snake.

"How did it get all these bites on its rear end?" she asked.

"Bites?" the man said.

"It's got bites all over its rear end. Somebody been fighting this dog?" Bonnie questioned.

"No, I don't fight him, that's a show dog," the man said.

"Alright, listen. I'm going to be nice, but please don't let me come here and ever see a dog that's been fought." Bonnie's tone was stern.

"Well I can show you the paperwork," the man started getting defensive.

"The paperwork's got nothing to do with all them marks, and maybe he had them before you got him, I'm not accusing you, don't get me wrong. But see he's got bite marks all over his back from where somebody had him.

"I better not catch nobody round here fighting no dogs." Bonnie told the man that it's against not only the law, but also God's law.

"And your name was what, sir?" she asked.

"Cedric Williams," he said.

"Yeah, I met you before." Bonnie made it clear that she would remember their visit, just like she remembered Cedric's Australian Shepherd. She would remember him and he would remember her.

I lowered my camera as Bonnie walked back toward the vehicle. She looked annoyed when she climbed in.

"I didn't call you because I didn't think it was stuff you needed to really get footage of, but one of those dogs has been fought at some point in time because he's got old scars on his back legs, and I just jumped his case. You'll hear it on the recorder.

"Same old, same old. I see this crap all the time. But what I'm looking for is fresh blood."

"Ya'll got a couple dollars?" We were gassing up next to a couple of brown baggers bumping their rap music. They asked Bonnie for some money.

"You ask me for two and I'll ask you for four," Bonnie laughed.

It was Martin Luther King Jr. Day, and the black man tried to guilt Bonnie into giving him money in the name of equality. It pissed Bonnie off, so she floored the gas pedal and peeled out of the parking lot. I looked in the rearview mirror as the men eyed us. I was nervous but felt safe with Bonnie. She doesn't have time for bullshit and she keeps a loaded revolver in her center console.

"You just want to jerk a knot in these people's tail." Bonnie took a bite from a granola bar. "You can't do that legally because if I do the wrong thing, they'll turn around and have me in court."

Best to just peel out and leave them in the dust.

We nosed through more backcountry roads. Bonnie rescued a bluenose pit bull puppy that had a big wound on the side of its face, and then she walked back into the woods near the house of man who was "notorious for fighting."

"I tell you what I'm going to do guys. I want you all to stay in the car, I'm going to walk across here. I don't know whose property it is, and right now, honestly I don't care." Bonnie pocketed her revolver and began traipsing around behind a doublewide trailer.

"The balls on that lady," Joe said as we watched Bonnie knock on the trailer door. She had a short conversation with a woman and then began walking back to the vehicle. I hit the record button on my camera so I would be ready to capture what she had to report.

"What I was doing guys, I was looking, because I saw two pits in the woods." Bonnie said the woman she was talking to was the sister of a man Bonnie took to court on charges of animal abuse. The woman, Bonnie said, would alert the neighborhood that Bonnie was out investigating, which meant dogs would be hidden and illegal activity halted for the day.

Most of the time Bonnie doesn't have enough evidence to bring charges, but her presence alone is enough to force pit fighters to think twice. Word travels quickly when Bonnie is on the hunt.

"It's a little bit hard to get into a pit bull fighting ring, because this is organized crime, highly organized crime. They don't want you to get in there.

"There's big money bet on these dog fights, and it's rampant in all of these little southern counties." Bonnie said if a person is not a fighter, they are probably a backyard breeder, trying to score some extra cash. And if they can't sell the dogs, they get rid of them in other ways.

"If they didn't want the dog to hang around, you just throw boiling water on the dog." Abusing a dog in this way, Bonnie said, is referred to as scalding. "I have found more scalded dogs in this county. I've had people call me up and say 'If you don't come and get this dog, I'm going to scald it.'"

We were starting to understand the hierarchy of animal abuse and dog fighting, which is very similar to that of the drug community. It's a cultural system that has plagued Greene County's reputation.

"When you have got a county full of pit bull fighters—and I mean full—no industry is going to want to come in there. Who is going to want to locate in a county where they have a pit bull-fighting, drug-dealing reputation?" Bonnie said the drug dealing and dog fighting go hand in hand, and where there are drugs, there is stealing and other petty crime.

"You better not turn your back in this county, unless you've got—like I do—a heck of an alarm system, like 20 something dogs that might eat somebody's lunch."

We pulled into the driveway of Mr. Scott, an older man that Bonnie knew from previous animal abuse cases.

It annoyed me that everyone in the South was addressed with a courtesy title. The last time I addressed someone as a 'Mr.' was in junior high school. It just seemed fake and unearned. We slowly picked up on the importance of saying, 'yes, ma'am,' and, 'thank you, sir' but it felt phony.

Again, Bonnie told us to stay in the car until she gave us the green light, something that had yet to happen. I was starting to wonder if we would ever get close up footage of Bonnie's interactions.

We watched her snoop around Mr. Scott's yard. There were dogs attached to chains all along the perimeter of the property, each had a turned-over barrel for shelter. Joe and I tried counting the ones we could see as Bonnie had what looked to be a heated conversation with Mr. Scott.

I spotted a sickly looking pit bull lying in the backseat of an old, rusted sedan that had no side door and was slowly becoming a fixture of the ground beneath it. I had a feeling we were finally onto something.

Bonnie's head was down as she made her way back to the vehicle. She didn't look happy. Finally, she tagged us in, telling us to follow her with our cameras.

Mr. Scott was standing by a pretty, brown pit bull with markings of white under its face and belly. It was attached to a thick rope.

"Alright, Dave. Look, get a picture of that," Bonnie said as Mr. Scott flipped the dog onto its back, revealing a tangled mess of blood, flesh and rope. It's what Bonnie explained to us as an embedded collar. The rope was too tight and had not been removed for so long that it cut into the dog's neck.

I zoomed in on the wound just before Bonnie pulled back on the rope, revealing folds of pink flesh. The rope was saturated with blood.

"It's grown into his neck, look," Bonnie said.

"It's not growing into his neck, I'm telling you he's only been over here four days." Mr. Scott was like a little kid who just pooped his pants but wouldn't admit to it even though there was shit running down his leg.

Bonnie breathed in hard through her nose with anger.

"Sir, look at the dog's neck." Bonnie pulled back on the rope again so he could see the wound. Mr. Scott tried to explain himself again but Bonnie had heard enough.

"Now wait Mr. Scott. Just let me talk to you a minute, okay?" she said. "I'm going to be real nice to you about it, but look here. Think about it, sir. What if *you* were out here on this rope and it was digging into *your* neck? That wouldn't be …"

"Listen to me." Mr. Scott interrupted again.

"I done come and find two of 'em dead up in the barrel, starved to death and froze!" Bonnie raised her voice to remind him of the last time she was on his property.

Mr. Scott tried explaining how he only had the dog tied up for four days. Prior to that, it was tied to the back of his truck. For some reason, he thought that information mattered and somehow diluted the severity of the crime.

Bonnie gave him two options: Sign over ownership of the dog to her or go to court.

Mr. Scott turned away from her, clearly upset. I didn't understand why he cared to keep the dog since he obviously gave it no attention and let it bleed out in his yard. But then again, nothing we had witnessed in Alabama the Beautiful made much sense to begin with.

The dog's injury gave off a rotten stench that made me gag. I tried holding my breath in spurts as I focused my camera on Bonnie, then the dog, and then Mr. Scott, trying to cover the interaction with fast-moving camera tricks like they do on Cops or TMZ.

"I'm going to be nice to you and give you a chance, whatever you'd like to do," Bonnie said.

After Bonnie laid out the logic in her argument, Mr. Scott finally gave in.

"Take him," he said.

"Yes, sir. He'll be in better hands." Bonnie's clever admonishment made me smile. She was so good at telling people to fuck off without actually having to say those words.

"I am going to tell you this," Bonnie said. "If I ever come back and see another dog in these kind of conditions ... sir, I'm going to get a warrant for your arrest. Is that fair enough?"

"Yes, ma'am," Mr. Scott said.

hen Bonnie reached out to shake his hand.

"What's your name?" Mr. Scott asked.

"I'm Bonnie Miller. I'm a fair lady, okay? I'm a fair lady."

Not a mile further down the road, Bonnie introduced us to Javalyn Wilson, a college student at the University of Alabama who was related to Mr. Scott.

Javalyn helps Bonnie. She's a rescuer and criminal informant in a way. Bonnie said Javalyn is the exception in Greene County: She's educated and able to understand how the culture where she grew up is harmful to society.

"I live in Forkland, Alabama," Javalyn said. "It's just a small little region down in the deep, deep south. I happen to see a lot. It's my senior year at the University of Alabama so I don't have as much time as I usually would to tend to animals around the neighborhood, but I witness a lot of neglect and starving animals. At one point I would go around the neighborhood with a bag of dog food and do the best I could.

"Once I had a job at Pizza Hut in Demopolis. I would take the leftover pizza or whatever was left over from the bar and I would go around and just feed strays and dogs that just wasn't being fed."

I asked her what she thought of Bonnie.

"For a long time I didn't even know about her, so finding out that there was at least just one person around our area that cared enough, and you know was actually out doing these types of things for our animals, it was just great.

"I commend her. I adore her. She knows that." Javalyn looked at Bonnie, smiled, and laughed happily.

I felt bad for Joe because he was sitting in the backseat close to Mr. Scott's dog, which smelled absolutely terrible. We rolled the windows down and Joe lit a cigarette. It was one of the only times I actually enjoyed the smell of tobacco, because it masked the less favorable smell of rotting animal flesh.

I assumed we were done for the day, but the sun wasn't quite down so Bonnie kept poking around neighborhoods.

"Nice to have some company, guys," Bonnie said. "Truly is, you know, because usually I'm doing this all by myself believe it or not."

Bonnie has no immediate backup in the field. She has no partner, nobody to watch her back. Her dad is convinced she will end up dead in a ditch someday. Her husband, Tim, however, isn't worried.

"She knows the line, she knows where not to cross, she knows where to stop," Tim said. "Am I jumping up and down doing cartwheels all the time? No. But I don't come in and jump up and down at what she's doing ... I'm not going to do that.

"She knows how to talk to people. She knows how to do these things. She knows the correct way to do it. You just don't go in there with guns blazing all the time. I'm not saying she wouldn't like to do that, but, anyway."

"Let's see what we got here." Bonnie put the SUV in reverse so she could pull up to another trailer home. "When we go in here kinda keep your camera down if you don't mind, unless we see something, because I can always say that I'm looking for so and so or I'm lost."

It wasn't long before Bonnie gave us the green light again. She was talking to Leon, the owner of several pit bulls. She told him about Mr. Scott's dog and how she threatened to take him to court if he didn't start respecting his animals. We followed her as she walked with Leon to his backyard.

"Who made the red birdhouse?" Bonnie asked, observing the birdhouse hanging in Leon's front yard.

"I did," Leon said.

"No joke!" Bonnie was showing interest in the man, trying to see the good in him even though he had starving dogs on his property. Just as Tim said, she knows how to talk to people.

"I wish you could make me a red birdhouse like that," she said.

Leon's backyard was covered in a makeshift kennel that sprawled from one end of the property to the other. It was pieced together by scrap wood, old signs and wire. The kennels were full of pit bulls, and more dogs were chained up at the tree line. There was garbage everywhere.

Bonnie leaned over the fence and pointed out ways Leon could better care for his animals. One dog had wire wrapped around its collar, which was poking into the dog's neck. She told him to remove the wire and tie up the dog properly.

I positioned my camera on the top of the fence, focused on a loop of barbed wire, and then smoothly moved the focus onto Leon, who was fielding more questions from Bonnie.

"What's up with the teddy bear?" Bonnie pointed to a big stuffed animal that was hanging from a rope above one of the dog kennels.

She walked along the fence and knelt down to greet a female dog whose head was weighed down by a large tractor chain.

"See, she's way too thin and she ain't got no straw, no nothing up in her house." Bonnie let the dog lick her fingers through the fence. She knew something was going on and was easing her way into a conversation about pit fighting.

She asked Leon about his neighbors and his children.

"You don't let them fight these pits do you?" she asked, not directly blaming Leon for what she knew was happening on his property.

"No, no. I ain't growing them up in that," Leon said.

"Teach 'em better, teach 'em better, man," Bonnie said. "You know what's wrong around this part of the country to me? People don't teach these kids good things, and then they end up in jail, in prison, and they wonder why.

"Anything that you let your kids do that's against the law ... then you can't say a word when they end up in prison."

Bonnie was clever and safe in how she conducted herself.

I trailed behind Leon as he led us around the back of the kennel. I wanted to punch him in the back of the head for being such and idiot, but asked him a question instead.

"You ever fight dogs when you were younger?" I asked.

Leon turned around, surprised to hear me speak for the first time.

"Coming up in my younger days, I did." Leon was stuttering terribly, and I could tell he was on drugs: He was missing teeth and his eyes floated in his skull as if unattached. "And I don't just fight 'em you know what I'm saying?"

I had no idea what he was saying, but I got the idea: he was breeding pit bulls, teaching them to attack giant teddy bears and selling them to fighting rings. Somewhere in the operation were drugs, too. I didn't need the blueprints; it was too damn obvious where I was.

"You turn a little bit older," he said, casually referring to growing out of the pit bull fighting ring, as if it were a phase in life, like when teenagers go through changes in their clothing style and music preferences.

He turned around again to follow Bonnie, and I prayed like hell that he would threaten her so I could knock him out cold. One hit. Job done. Fuck this guy.

Instead, he played dumb, knowing Bonnie couldn't charge him with anything unless there was fresh blood or he was in the act of abusing an animal. So Bonnie complimented him on his birdhouse again and we piled back in the car.

"You honestly never know what you're going to get into, so you have to be careful.

"If the situation looks too dangerous, I know when to back off," Bonnie said. "I'm one lady out here. Yeah I'm armed, but that doesn't mean anything if you're surrounded by idiots."

When we pulled into Bonnie's driveway, her vehicle was full of newly rescued animals, all of which would need to be vetted. Bonnie planned to bring them to Demopolis the next day.

Tim was tending to the kennels. He had just returned home from work and had yet to go inside the house. We all crammed into their shed where Tim slipped on latex gloves to give the dogs shots.

"I think I can sum it up this way," he said. "I can understand ignorance, but I cannot understand stupidity." He paused, looked at me, then at Joe. "Is that plain enough?

"Someone who doesn't know what to do ... that's different. But that's not the case here. People know what to do and they just don't do it because they don't care. So what you have then is what you've seen today, what *we* have to see every day, what my *wife* sees every day.

"Change laws, education would help. I'm not saying there's solvability to it all, but it would help. You can't just go out here and point your finger at it and say 'do this, do this.' There has to be laws, then there has to be enforcement of the laws."

I created a new file on my computer and labeled it 'Day 12,' our last scheduled day in Alabama. We woke early and drove to Eutaw where we hoped to speak with a law enforcement official about animal abuse and neglect in Greene County.

When we pulled up to the government building, we rounded the corner to find a spot to park where Joe could smoke a joint undetected. We saw a few stray dogs run through the lot of grass behind the building and disappear into the woods.

I walked into city hall without a name in my reporter's notebook.

"Can I help you?" a lady behind a glassed-in reception area leaned over her desk, catching me as I tried walking straight back to the administrative offices.

I told her I was hoping to speak with the chief of police. To my surprise, she picked up her phone, shared a few words with someone on the other end, then turned to me and said Chief Coleman's office is halfway down the hall on the left.

I ran out to grab Joe and the rest of our camera equipment before meeting Chief Coleman in his office. He's a tall black man and was very welcoming. We told him we had been following Bonnie Miller and were looking for a comment on the animal control issue in Greene County.

"Unfortunately we don't have anything in place here ... but we do have an independent person who goes out of her way to help us," Chief Coleman said, referring to Bonnie.

"If we do have an issue with animal cruelty or sick animals that's running astray or anything, we'll call on her and she'll come a running.

"To me, she's just the best person around. 'Cause like I said, she doesn't have to do this and she's always telling me how her husband is fussing because she took another dog in and they got to buy food.

"For her to take in these animals and feed them out of her pocket, that's big, that's real big," he said.

"How hard is it to enforce animal cruelty?" I asked.

"It's not really hard to enforce it," Chief Coleman said. "We do have laws in place in the state of Alabama so it's not a big issue on enforcing it. If we do have an incident that arises, we do have laws in place. It's just a matter of proving it, you know, proving what's going on and getting the evidence we need to charge them on it."

"If it's not too hard to enforce, then why do you think Bonnie is doing most of the work unpaid?" I asked.

"You know." Chief Coleman took a deep breath and rubbed his hands together. "Good question."

It was the last quote of our trip, and as we left Alabama, it made us think about what we had filmed and how we would use the material to tell the story of animal rescue in Alabama. In the end, all we really had—as Chief Coleman said—was a good question. Why is this happening? Why are people like Bonnie, Bobbi and Robbie used as a crutch by government and by the greater population of Alabama?

"That's just the way it's done here," Chief Coleman said.

We had the windows rolled down in the vehicle to keep us cool, but at the expense of our hearing. Joe used rubber bands to pin his dreadlocks against the sides of his head, protecting his ears from the air vacuum. As we sped across the Alabama state line into Mississippi, our communication was loud and brief.

"Fuck Alabama!" Joe screamed, drumming his fingers on the steering wheel to the rhythm of a Wide Spread Panic recording.

We cheered, cussed and sped up, thankful to be heading back to Minnesota and leaving the "shithole" behind us.

We laughed as we drove through the northeast corner of Mississippi, remembering what we had been told about the

Alabama motto "Thank God for Mississippi," because if it weren't for it's neighboring state, which is also plagued with animal abuse and drugs, Alabama would be the worst state to live in.

They really set the bar high, I thought.

But we weren't just leaving an undesired place; we were leaving behind the wonderful people who were fighting to improve that place. We were leaving behind Bonnie. We were leaving behind Tim. We were leaving behind Bobbi, Robbie and Kim. And thinking about that made us realize the plight and neglect is felt not only by the animals but also the rescuers.

And to that end, we knew our job wasn't done.

PART TWO
ONWARD

We left Alabama at a mild 50 degrees. I was wearing the same blue shorts I wore for the majority of our trip, a short sleeve button up shirt, and Keen sandals. My head was burrowed in a giant body pillow that I stuffed between the door and the passenger seat. Sunflower shells, empty water bottles and food wrappers littered the cup holders and dashboard trays.

Before making it home to Duluth, we stopped in Fargo, North Dakota, to return the vehicle we borrowed from Joe's dad. The temperature had already plummeted below zero as we pulled off at a rest area in South Dakota.

I opened the car door and cold air poured in, tangling around my ankles and prickling my feet like a bundle of needles. I ran into the building with my hands in my pockets, elbows pulled in at my sides, and chin tucked down to my chest, like a turtle retreating to its shell. It's a unique style of walking that all Minnesotan's know with intimacy. I took a few jolted gulps of cold air and felt my lungs seize up.

I thought about the correlation between weather and crime. Working as a part-time photographer at the television news station in Duluth, I learned that when spring hits, there would be more crime to report as people emerge from their homes and begin to mingle outside again. Maybe that's what Alabama needed: a good dose of below-zero weather to keep everyone indoors and out of trouble.

We drove through the night and were determined to push through the final few hours of frosted North Dakota fields. I dozed off periodically but tried to stay awake to help Joe stay alert at the wheel: our buddy system. We would make conversation without further purpose than to keep each other awake.

Not surprisingly, Joe brought up his disdain for his hometown.

"It's built on a God-damned flood plain," he said, referring to Fargo, North Dakota where every Spring, crews work around the clock sandbagging low areas of the city that are most likely to flood.

My grandpa, who lives 100 miles west of Fargo, enjoys expressing the same disdain for the city for exactly the same reason. But what is done is done, and so the sandbagging and levy building will always be a part of Fargo's character. As outsiders, it's easy to point a finger and refer to everyone living in Fargo as stupid for knowingly building their homes where flooding occurs annually.

The reputation of a place can distract from all of its better qualities. Take Alabama for example: College football and dog fighting ... two reputations that precede Alabama and the majority of southern states. They, too, distract from the better qualities of the area.

I thought about reputations in regards to the documentary we were producing: Do I acknowledge Alabama's better qualities? Would I be fishing for a silver lining that simply doesn't exist? They were questions I couldn't answer yet, especially considering I hadn't slept since leaving the south.

My eyelids were heavy as I stared at the wall behind the urinal. I zipped up my fly, pushed down the flushing lever with the underside of my palm, washed up, and ran back out to the car in the same turtle-tucked fashion.

Joe and I often bicker about lighting and camera angles. We are two artists with two separate artistic visions. But when we arrived back in Duluth, we immediately agreed that we needed to return to Alabama to finish our pursuit of a story. There were too many loose ends, and we both felt we had only started to understand the implications of animal cruelty.

We created a Kickstarter—crowd-funding—campaign and solicited the help of our social media following to raise enough money to upgrade our audio equipment and spend 30 more days on the road in Alabama.

I was at work at the ABC broadcast news affiliate in Duluth, standing between the newsroom and editing booths, when my phone buzzed in my pocket. It was Joe telling me we had already raised $40 toward continuing our journey in the south. I smiled, slid my phone away, then grabbed a handful of scripts from the news producer's desk and retreated back into an editing booth to dutifully fulfill my assignments.

We had exactly 51 days to reach our fundraising goal, otherwise all pledges would become null and I would spend the upcoming summer slouched in an editing booth instead of chasing a true American story.

The subhead on our fundraising page read: "We are filming a documentary about the culture of animal cruelty in the south and the grassroots effort to change it." For the most part, southern residents thanked us for bringing the plight of animals and animal rescuers alike into public view, but when we received positive feedback, we knew the hate mail would be soon to follow.

Steve Johnson, an Alabama resident, seemed hell-bent on posting hyperbolic statements to our Facebook page with bad grammar and ill intent:

"It seems anyone with a camera and a battery charger can produce a 'documentary'. Here is a prime example, a local group from Minnesota decided to come to Alabama to 'document' animal abuse. The group is two guys and a video camera. Claiming to be journalist, they produced a video that claims everyone in Alabama is a toothless, ignorant, redneck that beats or eats their pets everyday. Hmmm, I know a few 'legitimate' journalist. You decide, it makes me mad that groups choose Alabama as an easy target."

When you can't drive from one city to the next without seeing a dead dog on the side of the road, Alabama becomes an easy target. Joe and I weren't interested in targeting a specific state, and we weren't ignorant to the truth of animal abuse being a nationwide problem; however, like Steve Johnson said, we were just two guys with limited resources, and so ... Alabama it was.

We allowed ourselves time to digest the comments flooding our Facebook page and Kickstarter inbox and learned that there are two types of people at work on the periphery of animal abuse: those who decide to turn a blind eye, and those working tirelessly to fix the problem. Our documentary, we decided, would aim to celebrate the work of those fighting against ignorance.

Joe and I were crammed into his bedroom preparing for a call with Oliver Bogner, executive producer at Bogner Entertainment, a Los Angeles-based production company focused on pitching television shows to networks like National Geographic and Animal Planet. Bogner found our Kickstarter campaign and was interested in transforming our project into a reality television show.

The idea made us hesitant for many reasons. We didn't want to glorify animal cruelty by means of reality television, and we were also concerned with losing the rights to our content, selling out and not being able to produce a documentary. "Sucking the corporate dick" as Joe delicately explained. But in the end, we came to the same conclusion as most Alabama animal rescuers: the more exposure the better. Maybe a reality television show could embarrass Alabama to the point where animal cruelty would take more of a front row in politics, leading to stricter laws and more enforcement. In a roundabout way, it might actually help advance animal welfare and urge people like Steve Johnson to re-evaluate their baseless state pride.

So we took the call.

Mr. Bogner's voice was hurried and muffled by wind. I imagined him shuffling across a busy L.A. street, business portfolio in one hand, latte in the other, cell phone tucked between his shoulder and cheek, and two or three assistants in close tow. I had never been to California and never spoken with anyone in the entertainment business, but I felt my imagination wasn't far off.

We gave Bogner a sense of the story we were following, and relayed to him the feedback—good and bad—that our project was receiving. Ultimately, we told him our goal was to help alleviate the emotional and financial burden animal rescuers in the south are saddled with. If a reality television show could advance our goal, then we were all ears.

"Do you know the difference between reality television and documentary?" Bogner asked.

He wasn't interested in documentary style, let alone a true story. He wanted drama.

With reality television, he said, you have to "create action."

We explained to Bogner that the action was already happening, and to force it wouldn't be necessary. The subjects we were filming had character and naturally dramatic lives. He seemed interested and told us to edit together some of our best footage into a sizzle reel and he would run it by his colleagues.

Joe and I walked to a local burrito joint to discuss a course of action over locally brewed beer. The snow had mostly melted and the sun was hot in the sky. We were finally absorbing vitamin D again, and after a promising conversation with Bogner, we were giddy with excitement.

Burrito Union is unique in its Soviet-themed décor and features burritos like the Imperial Chicken and Fat Capitalist, which was ironic since we were there to discuss the moral imperatives of selling an originally journalistic endeavor as a reality television show.

I ordered a Fat Capitalist and an Apricot Wheat beer, brewed just down the hill at Fitger's Brewhouse. The homegrown feel, along with its proximity to the beautiful Chester Creek, made Burrito Union our go-to place for food and beer.

Spencer, a popular bartender, pulled back a blown-glass beer tap in front of me and filled our beer glasses. Joe and I were in our "happy place." Drinking good beer, eating good food, and discussing the possibility of selling a reality television show to a major network. Not a bad day.

We decided we needed to hire a lawyer to look over contracts from Bogner's office. Joe's uncle, a photography agent, knew of a lawyer specializing in entertainment and put us in contact. He would cost us $500 an hour but would be worth it in the end.

We fantasized about the potential of our project and reveled in the momentum it was building. Feeling the need to celebrate, we ordered another beer.

My feet were tapping on the bar rail under our stools. Post-graduate life finally felt like it was moving somewhere, and I couldn't wait for it to move faster. The project was taking hold online, we were getting calls from Beverly Hills area codes, and our Kickstarter was reaching its monetary goal. The dream of becoming a backpack journalist was coming into focus.

We sat in silence, staring at the television screens above the bar and soaking in the excitement of the day.

"Life is a rollercoaster," Joe said, manifesting a romantic perspective on life.

I knew exactly how he felt, holding his hit and waiting for life to happen and knock him off his bar stool.

As liberal arts majors, Joe and I are plagued with a tendency to see life from afar, to witness the hills and valleys of our collective narratives. But at that moment, I felt like I was destined for nothing but smooth sailing.

I sent my girlfriend a text message saying I had good news to share with her. She had just returned from a spring break service trip and I was excited to catch her up on our conversations with Bogner and the early success of our Kickstarter campaign. I was also eager to learn about her trip.

When she was gone, she sent me a message saying, "We need to talk," which I tried not to overthink, but deep down, I was concerned.

We were living together at the time, and when she returned from her trip, she didn't come home; instead, she was staying at her mother's home and avoiding contact with me. I had no idea what was going on with her. Maybe some good news on my end would get her talking.

Joe and I paid our tabs and grabbed complimentary mints on our way out. Since nice days are hard to come by in Duluth, we decided to go for a hike along Chester Creek.

A half mile into our hike, my girlfriend and a guy from her spring trip went running by Joe and I in the opposite direction. We hadn't seen each other in over a week, and when she ran by, she waved at me shyly like I was a distant acquaintance. Both she and the guy she was with exhibited the behavior of guilty dogs trying to avoid eye contact after shitting on the family room carpet.

And just like that, life happened and knocked me off my barstool.

"I'm sorry," Joe said.

I grinned nervously, thinking of what Joe had said minutes ago about life being a rollercoaster. Then the tears pooled in the corners of my eyes and I struggled to understand what emotion I was feeling. Anger and sadness were at opposition and I felt as if that rollercoaster would never emerge from its new low.

"Onward," Joe said, with the same brevity he always used during tense situations.

Onward, I thought.

Life goes on. Find a row and hoe it.

My full attention was now on getting back to Alabama to continue pursuit of the story.

BOYHOOD BLUES

I CREATED A FOLDER ON MY COMPUTER'S DESKTOP labeled 'Alabama.' It's where I kept animal related news clippings and photos. That morning, I was tagged in a story on Facebook about a group of young Alabama boys who stuffed a dog's mouth with fire crackers, taped its mouth shut and lit the fuse, blowing off the animals snout and burning the majority of its face all in the name of fun, and likely, boredom.

I winced at the image, then dragged it from Facebook and dumped it into the Alabama folder. When I told Joe about it later that day, he said he started blocking certain animal rescuers from his Facebook because he was tired of seeing pictures of dead animals.

At the time, I wasn't feeling much of anything. I was busy mending the damage done by a failed relationship and trying to find new routines and passions.

Where did the past three years go? I led myself down that dark road that had no end. But it was one I had to walk, so I clocked in and out for the next few weeks until little by little my cynicism and young naivety toward life began to wear away.

I was running along Tischer Creek—my new morning routine— when I began imaging that picture filed under the Alabama folder. I tried to recreate the events of that incident. I pictured myself as one of those young boys stuffing a dog's mouth with firecrackers. I wondered if they felt remorse after the dog's face was split in half.

Then, I replayed an incident from my childhood when I inflicted pain on another individual and couldn't help but ask myself what made me so much different than those young animal abusing boys in the deep south.

No matter how many promises I made before my father gave in and bought a five horsepower motor for our small aluminum boat, he had to know there were some promises I could not keep. Any 15-year-old, hormone-heavy teenager will find a way to make a mistake. Risk taken.

"David, your life jacket," my father motioned toward the fluorescent Stearns vest splayed out on the dock reminding me of a hopeless fish. Stearns, my father explained, was a local company. But that didn't concern me. I didn't know about global economics and the exportation of labor. All I knew was Central Minnesota ... and I barely knew that.

"I know Dad, geez." I thought if he noticed my annoyance he would stop badgering me, but my response only welcomed more admonishment.

"Never forget to put it on, it's important. All it takes is you bonking your head and falling in. People die that way."

Somehow the threat of death always worked, but the idea of dying felt foreign, so I continued to question the motive by which my father used it freely to teach me lessons of safety.

"Alright, alright," I said and swung the jacket around my body, carefully pressing the buckles together as to not pinch my fingers between the clasps. Little blood blisters seemed to be the only thing that life jacket gave me.

Click.

With an eye of concentration, my father lowered the gas can over the funnel I held for him. As he poured, specks of gas inevitably found their way to the water and exploded into rainbows across the surface, something only chemists and people like my father understood but I could only gaze at in amazement, starry-eyed and stupid.

I kept a steady hand on the funnel and watched as the sleeve of my father's Patagonia fleece slid up his arm revealing muscles I didn't know he had, expanding and overflowing under his dark arm hair like a wild river. He was never one to wear his accomplishments on his sleeve, and just like he hid his muscles under his fleece, he possessed deep knowledge, vast reserves from years of experiences, knowledge I could only hope to someday understand. Without intention, he taught me that power is the quiet possession of knowledge and strength.

After showing me how to squeeze the bulb, choke the engine and connect the kill switch, my father finally sent me on my way, kicking the nose of the boat away from the dock with what I imagine was great hesitation.

The boat rattled like a lawn mower as I opened the throttle over Long Lake. Such a racket made it hard to go unnoticed. Lithe, browning bodies shifted slightly on their beach towels, rubbernecking, trying to catch a glimpse of the noise interrupting their pampered peace. I felt like Holden Caulfield exploring the world for the first time. Exploring it alone.

Yet my father wasn't far behind, perched at the end of the dock in his bright orange fleece, the one my mother and I teased him for wearing. The one my sister was convinced he wore simply to embarrass us in public.

I could feel his eyes behind me. Burning on my shoulders like two slants of July sun. I felt like a squirrel scattering behind a tree as I pushed the throttle down to round the bend as fast as possible and be out of his sight.

What is he thinking? Is he proud? Nervous?

Don't look back. Show him you know what you're doing, that you're capable of controlling the boat on your own.

I could never fully understand my father, and I liked it that way. His quiet, mysterious demeanor was puzzling. His actions were always absolute, like he knew exactly what he was doing, like he knew he was right. Confidence, I thought. But his emotions never peaked. He never showed too much, never gave much away. It made him hard to crack, irritating and irresistible as a role model.

The wind was in my face, sun in my eyes, and every turn of the engine shook the hull and consequently my entire body, sending a tingling sensation across my skin. Vibrations of freedom, I thought. Felt good.

The fish, I imagine, knew when I was coming to find them. Nothing and nobody could avoid hearing the fresh motor roar within its plastic shell, especially me. In fact, I was thriving on it, trying to force the throttle beyond its threshold to release every bit of juice it had, thinking if I pushed it past its breaking point it would somehow release more horsepower. But I knew nothing about motors and nothing about horsepower. I was screaming across Long Lake in Central Minnesota, in a place I knew nothing about. I was experiencing my first portion of the delicate taste of responsibility, hopping on a horse for the first time, kicking it from a trot to a gallop. Knowing nothing about how to control the reigns.

Long Lake is named well, spanning ten times long as it is wide. It can be mistaken for a landing strip to aircrafts above. It's the color of watered-down pea soup and sits 25 feet deep in the middle. Its waters only stretch one mile, yet further than my small, childhood existence.

Skirted with houses, it's a recreational hub. Waterskiers populate the long stretches down the middle, while fisherman and canoeists work the periphery. Jet skiers zig and zag in tight circles like drunk water bugs, trying to stir up big waves. My mom always hated the monotonous drone of their engines. I never told her I thought they were cool and would jump on the back of one if I ever got the chance. Contradicting my mom's opinion was dangerous. I had watched my sister do it plenty of times and knew better. Similar to my father, my mother was like an omniscient reader, somehow able to know exactly what I was thinking. Like how when I yawned, it meant I was nervous.

Long Lake looked different to me that day. Everything, I imagined, looks different from the helm, more controllable. There was a time when I stuck to the shoreline, working my paddleboat in and out of lily pads while hunting largemouth bass with plastic frogs, mainly because my father warned me of all the "knuckleheads" boating aimlessly and dangerously on the lake. But this day was different; I pointed the boat straight to the center, barely able to see over the bow as the boat struggled to get on a plane. Without clear direction, I was somehow confident in where I was going.

I let the boat level to trolling speed as I reached the lake's sandbar, a popular swimming and fishing spot. If you're careful and your timing is right, you can safely wade across the lake along a ribbon of sand, something my father advised against. Now I was on my own and the decision was mine. I could wade to the middle of the sandbar as boats screamed past on either side. I could taunt and tease, flail my arms and flaunt my freedom. But that's not what I was there for. I was there to fish, or at least to craft a fishing story to carry proudly back to my father, one he would somehow know contained threads of fabrication, or was at least exaggerated to some extent. The story waiting to be played out, however, was not about a fish *this big* or about a *lunker* that snapped my line and got away. It was one of shame, one that would change my life forever.

It's really not that difficult. Even if you know nothing about fishing, your chances of catching a fish at the sandbar are good. I remember the first time I tried it. I was with my aunt and uncle. My uncle tied what he called a "popper" on the end of my line, the same lure he was using. It looked more like a tube of lipstick than a frog, but it was working well for my uncle so I didn't question his method. He showed me how to reel it in, jerking the rod downward so the mouth of the lure made a popping noise as it caught resistance along the surface of the water. That movement, he explained, will catch the attention of a largemouth bass and maybe a northern pike, two fish I knew nothing about but had me excited anyway.

I hurled the lure as far as I could, but instead of taking my uncles advice, I just let it sit there. I watched the lure bob in and out of the swells between waves for a good 20 minutes before a fish slurped it in. It was my first catch on Long Lake and it was an easy one.

There was also the time when I went swimming with my neighbor, Alex, and his mother, Judy. Alex and I put on goggles and chased sunfish with nets while Judy sat chest deep in the water taking in the sun. Alex and I were honed in on a sunfish. We were both underwater drifting slowly toward it with our nets, Alex from behind and me from the front. Half of the fun was plotting our attack, like two Navy admirals bent over a map discussing strategy. We were in "stealth mode." We didn't know exactly what that meant but had heard the phrase on TV and liked the sound of it. Our cheeks were full of air and our nets were inching closer to the sunfish when I heard a muffled cry from above the surface.

I slowly backed away from the sunfish before surfacing to see what had happened. Alex emerged in the same manner. We both slipped off our goggles, revealing big red circles around our eyes as Judy tried to contain her laughter long enough to tell us that a sunfish bit the mole on her back.

Yes, it really is that easy to attract a fish at the sandbar. But over the years I had learned how to go about it most efficiently, how to pitch a spinner bait or plastic worm on the weed line and how to work the lure so it appears more realistic. So when I pulled up to the sandbar and cut the motor, I wasn't hoping to catch just one fish, but to set a new personal record and do it alone.

I wasn't surprised to see Greg Anderson in his blue paddleboat working the weed line. His two sisters were perched in the back, attentively watching their big brother fish.

Greg and I attended school together beginning in elementary. We were both in middle school at the time, but I didn't see him often because he was in a class of students who required extra attention. He was on the receiving end of many jokes and pranks. When I was really young I never played along in teasing him, simply because I was too shy to even try. But now, braced with my 5hp motor and aluminum boat, I was more confident than ever and decided to push that newfound confidence to its limits.

Zinggg.

I let my spinner bait fly toward Greg and his sisters. I was confident in my casting abilities and decided to give them a scare by landing my lure as close to their paddleboat as possible, before closing the bail and letting the lure fall inches short of their boat.

"What the heck!" Greg yelled as he rose from a ducking position. His sisters appeared frightened as they turned toward Greg for reassurance that they were safe and that I was only joking. Greg just smiled at me.

"What's up, Dave?" he said as he reeled in his line, jerking his rod from side to side to make his lure appear more alive as it swam toward him and his sisters like a snake.

Greg didn't appear to be upset. He was accustomed to bullying, so he just laughed and smiled at me, continuing to jerk his rod back and forth with anticipation. It was almost like he was expecting it. Like he assumed everyone around him would eventually try to push his buttons. He was only 15 years old and already immune to assholes.

I didn't say anything. I was suddenly feeling inferior, just like I had with my father as he chided me for not listening when he explained how the motor takes a mixture of gas and oil. I started to feel anxious, helplessly watching all the confidence I had bolstered moments ago dry up in the sun. I stared out across the water and realized my lure had sunk to the bottom, and just like my newly found independence, needed to be reeled back in.

With one knee cushioned on the back seat and the opposite foot braced against the back of the boat, I steadied myself before pulling back on the rope that somehow kicks the motor into life. I vaguely remember my father explaining how it worked or what it was called. I was pulling back on the thing connected to the other thing that made the big thing start, knowing nothing about how any of those things worked.

After a few strong pulls, the motor erupted and roared to life, spitting out a thick cloud of smoke that stung my eyes. I thought about what my father would say, how the smoke meant that I squeezed the bulb too many times and flooded the engine. I was out of his sight but could see him stationed at the end of the dock in his bright orange fleece and omniscient point of view, listening to the heavy cough of the motor and somehow knowing exactly what I had done. What I did next, however, was beyond his imagination.

I wasn't thinking. I pushed forth the throttle and aimed the boat at Greg. I could see over the bow just enough to realize I had his attention. He was yelling something as I closed in, but I couldn't hear anything over the clamoring motor. It wasn't a day for listening; it was a day for pushing limits.

I was trying to gauge how close I could get before turning, before smacking the aluminum hull into the side of Greg's paddleboat. I thought about ditching the whole idea and turning before I could even scare Greg and his sisters, but that wasn't an option. It wasn't a day for ditching efforts; it was a day of following through.

I remembered my sister's physics book, the one that showed an object traveling at the speed of X and how she had to determine, based on other variables, how fast that object was traveling. I remembered her arguing with my father as he tried to explain the equation. I remembered feeling scared about going to high school and enrolling in that class, carrying around big books and working out equations in college-ruled notepads. Those things frightened me. All I knew was that I was going fast and was faced with a problem that no equation could guide me through.

I never let off the throttle, even as Greg stood waving his arms. I plowed past the white and orange buoy bobbing twenty feet off shore at the sandbar, quickly turning in to one of the "knuckleheads" my father always warned me about. Those brief seconds before I decided to turn and bypass Greg seemed to last forever and the frightened look on Greg's face was burning hard into the back of my memory.

Many kids used their words to assert their superiority over Greg. Words like "retard" and "idiot." Words that did little to penetrate the shield he put up between himself and the world. At the time, I didn't think what I was doing would hurt him anymore than those words my schoolmates practiced on him.

I was able to turn the boat just before colliding with Greg and his sisters in what could have been a fatal accident. *Just a scare*, I thought. But it was more than that. It wasn't even about Greg. It was about my own damn insecurity. I was trying to decide what kind of person to be and how to be that person. I didn't want to be the kid who never spoke up, who never had the balls to take a dare or ask out a girl. I wanted to know what it meant to be confident. I didn't realize it at the time, but Greg was the only person who could show me what it truly meant to walk with confidence.

The sun beat down hard, but not as hard as the realization of what I had just done. Scaring Greg was supposed to make me smile and laugh like the other kids who teased him. Instead I felt strained, like I was trying to lift a heavy weight off the ground but it wouldn't budge. I felt like someone had squeezed my bulb too tight and consequently flooded my engine, rendering it useless. I felt like Holden Caulfield again. Not the Holden Caulfield who was exploring the world for the first time, but the one who had seen it and realized it wasn't what he expected it to be.

I couldn't think. All I could do was put the boat in cruise control and aim it back home. This time I didn't feel like pushing limits. I puttered along at snail pace, undetected by all the oiled bodies on their beach towels. I was like a ghost to them, drifting slowly to shore like some sort of dark plague.

Going home meant facing my parents. I didn't like the thought of it, so I took my time docking the boat, carefully attending to every detail my father rehearsed for me.

Walking through the steps of docking the boat drained me—not because they were hard to follow but because they reminded me of my father. How he stood sternly at the end of the dock, watching me cruise off into the distance. How he hesitated slightly before sending me off. How he somehow knew I was going to mess up the chance he gave me. How he let me go anyway.

I felt like a cowering dog as I walked back to the house. I was hoping my parents wouldn't find out what I did, that I had put someone's life in danger, that I did it intentionally. My gut was so tied up in guilt that I also hoped they would question it out of me, that they would somehow deduce it from my body language and provide my conscience some relief. I was afraid of being caught and not being caught, waiting in a self-loathing limbo.

I walked into the house and sat on the couch. My mother was cooking dinner, probably the next version of her jambalaya that she was working to perfect. I didn't bother looking; I just cowered my way into the living room.

Zoey, our family dog, was lying in a slant of sunshine that warmed the carpet. She's the only one that could lie around all day without reprimand. How easy life must be for her.

I was starting to feel sorry for myself. Zoey felt my presence and raised her head briefly off the ground, lazily assessing her environment. As she laid her head back down she kept her eyes one me. They were sad eyes. It seemed as though she was feeling sorry for me too. She either knew I was about to be reprimanded or she was the first one to figure out my new secret. If only Greg and my parents were as forgiving as her. Life, I was learning, was nothing like I expected it to be.

I didn't bother turning on the TV, nothing could distract me from my guilty conscience. My mother's jambalaya was making hot, oily noises in the pot, and I began to smell its mixture of flavors. Normally I would be impatiently raiding the cupboards for granola bars, fruit snacks, or anything to tide me over and bridge the 30 minutes between self-described starvation and dinnertime. I wasn't hungry this time. My stomach was tied in a knot, my hands were sweaty and my eyes were widely fixed on the bookcase next to the TV.

I read the titles of books my parents had acquired over the years. They were in no particular alphabetical or thematic order. Squeezed between a fat, historical account of the Civil War and a tall, slender picture book of famous architecture were a few Scrabble dictionaries. I wondered if they contained a word that could describe the new, downer sensation that was coursing through my body.

I stared at those books for what seemed an eternity, occasionally wetting my eyes with a blink. I stared at each individual title, then the wall of books as a collective mosaic. I pulled them in and out of focus, scanned them from left to right, then in the opposite direction. I thought if I read them I could understand my parents better and maybe be able to explain my actions to them. But I knew that wasn't possible. I knew my mother would ask me *what in the hell* I was thinking and I knew I would respond by saying I wasn't thinking at all. I knew she would ask me the same question again just to reinforce her anger. Much like the great leaders of the Civil War, the ones my father read about in his books, I knew what was coming. I just had to wait for it.

The phone rang a few times before my mother was able to dry off her hands on the kitchen rag to answer it. I was hoping it was my neighbor, Alex, asking me to come play video games and drink soda, things I was only able to do at his house. Usually I was capable of discerning who was on the other end of the line based on the subject of conversation, but this conversation seemed to be entirely one sided.

"I am so, so sorry, I will have a talking with him," my mother said. Her response seemed to be directed at me. I was facing away from her but I could feel her eyes on me. I suppose it was nice of her to give me fair warning of the inevitable lecture, but I didn't need warning. The minute I stepped off that boat I knew exactly what I was in for.

My mother hung up the phone gently, like she was paying her last respects to the caller who divulged my secret. My heart sank.

I've been in similar situations in the past: the brief moments before my parents issued my sentencing, before the judge's hammer came down to release me into the custody of my own dark conscience. Usually I would approach the bench and question the grounds on which I was being tried. This time was different, however. I wasn't trying to guess at which privileges would be revoked or how long I would have to sit in the isolation of my bedroom, forced to listen as the rest of my family had dinner without me. This time I turned myself in, but that didn't change the way my parents reacted.

"Who was that?" I asked my mother.

It wasn't a serious question. We both knew who it was and the information that was shared.

"Fuck ... fuck! You've got to be kidding me," she yelled as she stared at the floor, trying to decide how to handle the situation, how to reprimand her son.

My guilt was spreading like a bad virus. At first, I only felt guilt for having made a poor decision, but seeing how much I let my mother down added another level of emotional complexity. It reminded me of the line of domino's I set up as a kid, lined in patterns across the living room floor like a miniature army: once the first one fell, the rest followed, leaving a mess behind. I didn't know how long my line of guilt would spread before I would spend the time picking up the pieces. The first domino, however, had fallen fast.

My mother and I both knew that there was only one way she handled reprimand: whatever she felt, she said. She never wasted time glossing over her speech for imperfections. Whatever emotion boiled to the surface first, she ladled out and splashed across the room in violent patterns like a Ralph Steadman painting. Watching her anger rise was like staring down a 10-gauge shotgun with nowhere to hide. All I could do was wince and duck my head.

"What in the *hell* were you thinking? Fuck!"

My mother hollered and I stood there with nothing to say for myself. I didn't know where to look. I was like a submissive dog redirecting its attention to the ground, but that didn't even feel safe. My mother was controlling me and there was nothing I could do. I just stood there and let the guilt take over. My stomach was like the rock tumbler my father bought for my birthday, turning and mixing its insides in at a consistent speed. I just hoped whatever came of it would surprise me as much as those shiny, tumbled rocks.

My father was upstairs typing on his computer and listening to Sister Hazel. I remember those lyrics: *Everything is wonderful, everything's alright.* I remember the dark irony of that moment and my inability to escape it. Everything seemed terrible. Everything seemed to be working against me. If there was a God, he was controlling my environment in an orchestrated way, forcing me into some hypnosis and rendering my mind completely numb. Then the music from upstairs faded, the typing on the computer stopped and everything else began on cue.

"What's going on?" my father called down.

He was asking to be tagged into the fight, not because my mother needed relief, but because she had so much left in the tank he was worried she would explode unless she took a few minutes to cool down.

My mother yelled back up to him, explaining how I almost killed Greg and his sisters. She explained how Greg's mother, Gail, called to explain how terrified Greg's sisters were.

"Better call him and apologize," my father said.

"You bet your ass he's going to," my mother said as she handed me the phone.

I asked my mother what Greg's number was, a question I regretted immediately. She pointed to the thick, yellow phonebook and told me to figure it out for myself.

"Did you really just ask me that? Fuck! What's the matter with you?" my mother was still venting her anger.

"Pam, stop swearing," my father called down again.

She didn't listen to him; she kept saying exactly what was on her mind with the inflection of a ramped-up actor. My father went quiet. He knew the real issue at hand was his 15-year-old kid who not only almost killed his schoolmate but also had the balls to ask his mother to look up a number for him in the phone book. I was lucky she didn't pick up the heavy book and beat me over the head with it, something that was starting to sound preferable.

I flipped through pages and pages of people with the last name Anderson. It was surprising to find how many there were. Just the Andersons alone were more people than I imagined lived in Minnesota. But I didn't know anything about our state's population, let alone how to use a phone book.

I remember my mother telling me how her father was so strong he could tear a phone book in half. He died before I was born, so I never had the pleasure of seeing it for myself. I was becoming so anxious that I thought about giving it a try. But I wasn't the person my grandpa was, or at least the person he was described as being. I was 15 and weak in physical and mental strength, a premature, prepubescent teenager going through life like nothing mattered, like it was all a big joke.

The upstairs was still soundless and I wondered what my father was preparing for. His lectures were always methodical and structured like a thesis paper. Every argument would lead perfectly into the next, stringing together facts in a carefully articulated narrative explaining why my actions would not be tolerated. I didn't know what narrative my father was preparing but I knew that after I made my phone call, I could expect to be summoned upstairs for his delivery.

I was scanning through the phonebook slowly to delay the inevitable apology I was about to give. I had no idea what I would tell Greg other than the fact that I was sorry for what I did. I was starting to question what it really meant to be sorry. I've given apologies in the past, mainly because my mother demanded I do so. I made apologies because it's what I was *supposed* to do and because it was the only way to settle disputes and avoid further conflict.

When my index finger landed on Scott and Gail Anderson of 212 Long Lake Lane, my throat tensed up in fear. I let down Greg. I let down Greg's sisters. I let down my parents and now I was realizing that I let down Scott and Gail Anderson of 212 Long Lake Lane. My line of guilt was quickly growing longer, and all I felt was the fear of not knowing where it would end.

I picked up the phone. A dial tone buzzed through the receiver as I held the phone in front of me. Each time I entered a number, the phone responded with a beep, affirmation that the number had been recorded.

Beep, beep, beep.

Seconds were counting down before I would break the lump in my throat and muster out an apology.

Beep, beep, beep.

My hand started to shake and my stomach tumbled. The lump in my throat expanded and I wondered if I would be able to say what I needed to say.

Beep, beep, beep, beep.

I lifted the phone to my ear and listened to it ring. I thought about hanging up after the third ring and telling my mother nobody was home. Unlike the simple apologies I made in the past, this one felt complex and real. I was afraid to give an apology for the first time in my life and realized it was because I was truly sorry for what I did. It was my father who told me to apologize and my mother who dropped the phonebook in front of me. They had given me an order, but for the first time I wasn't complying to fulfill their request, I was making that phone call because somewhere in my own body I felt it was the right thing to do. If only that feeling came earlier when I aimed the boat at Greg and his sisters.

Everything is wonderful, everything's alright.

I didn't know who Sister Hazel was or why she thought everything was so damn wonderful.

"Hello," the voice on the other end of the line greeted me.

I didn't say who I was or why I was calling. I no longer enjoyed hearing my own name, knowing the reputation that it was now associated with. I just asked if Greg was available.

I could hear Greg's father calling for him. I tried to picture the scene. I imagined Greg behind a closed bedroom door, trying to make sense of what happened to him and his sisters on the lake. I imagined him wiping tears from his eyes and wondering why he deserved to be treated so poorly. I imagined him this way because I didn't want to lose that feeling of guilt, because I knew I deserved to feel guilty and never wanted to forget what it felt like to be truly sorry.

"Hello," Greg was now on the phone.

"Hi Greg, it's Dave," I said, not knowing what I would say next. Greg acknowledged me and waited to hear what I had to say.

"I just wanted to apologize for earlier. I'm sorry for teasing you and your sisters, it won't happen again."

Greg gave me his forgiveness and the conversation was over. It was over for Greg. It was over for my parents, and it was over for Scott and Gail of 212 Long Lake Lane. But it wasn't over for me. I didn't know what needed to happen for me to clear my conscience; in fact, I questioned whether it could ever be fully repaired. All I knew is that the conversation wasn't over. It was one I would have with myself repeatedly for years to come, one with no clear ending, a necessary conversation.

And there I was, coming down from my run along Tischer Creek, reliving the time I let my size and power take control of me, resulting in a scarring memory for Greg Anderson and his sisters. Having a necessary conversation with myself.

A lot had changed since then. I befriended Greg in high school, initially because I wanted to clear my conscience, but in the end he became a good friend and someone I truly cared about.

He called me that week to tell me he was going to a Minnesota Twins game and that I should watch for him on television. I told him I would. He asked me how I was doing, and I told him about filming the animal rescue documentary and about my failed relationship ... the good and the bad.

"She was stupid, anyway," Greg said.

I smiled and felt like crying, because after all of the years that passed since I teased Greg, I still couldn't forgive myself. Every time he called, every time he showed compassion toward me, that lump in my throat floated back up.

It made me think about those young boys in Alabama who blew up a dog's head with firecrackers. I wondered if there was a difference between them and my 15-year-old self. A chill came over me and I shuttered at the thought of it.

KISS THE PIG

Our fundraising campaign had plateaued and we began overanalyzing the content on our crowd-funding page:

Should we have worded it differently?

Did we make a mistake labeling animal abuse in the south as a culture?

Is the video too grotesque for people to watch?

Thinking ourselves in circles, we finally decided that we needed to find creative ways to push the Kickstarter along.

I leveraged my contacts at the ABC affiliate and got us a short feature on the 10 o'clock news. Joe reached out to a sorority at the University of Minnesota Duluth that was preparing for its annual Kiss the Pig fundraiser, where students nominate professors to kiss a pig. Each professor had a jar with their name on it, and students would put money in the jar of the professor they most wanted to see kiss a pig. That year, the sorority decided the fundraiser would benefit our documentary.

Students and faculty flooded the student center and a short speech was made about the event and our documentary. But all eyes were on the pig, which was being guided on a leash in the middle of the room.

The man giving the speech asked the group of professors who wanted to kiss the pig first. They looked at the pig, then at each other.

"I'll do it," I said, immediately regretting my attempt to break the awkward silence that had taken over the room. My thinking was that if professors of my alma mater were willing to kiss a pig to help me raise money to finish filming a documentary, then I damned well better be willing to get on my hands and knees to return the favor.

I squatted down by the pig and made a move toward it. He snorted and shuffled away from me and everyone laughed. My cheeks went red as I moved around the pig trying to determine where and how to kiss it.

As I got closer, I could see flaking skin tangled in the pig's coarse hair and my stomach tightened. I gave him a peck on the head and immediately wiped my mouth on my sleeve. Everyone laughed and cheered as I retreated to the edge of the crowd where Joe stood grinning at me. I knew I would never live that moment down.

My old journalism professor was next. He chose to sweet talk the pig before chasing it down for a kiss, which received a wild response from onlookers.

I watched as students walked by, craning their necks to see what the commotion was about. There were students walking toward the medical building, white lab coats floating behind them like those of doctors moving quickly down a hospital corridor. There were student athletes donning the school's insignia on their sleek jackets, walking out of class and to the field for practice. There were students of engineering, carrying loaded backpacks to their dorm rooms where they would study physics and math.

I watched those students walk confidently toward their future careers. As an English graduate, I wondered what path I was walking and where it would lead me. For now, I was kissing a pig to fund my endeavors. I felt slightly insecure not having a plan but was happy knowing there were people willing to help me succeed.

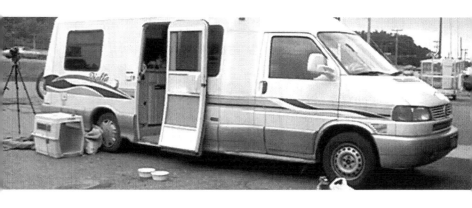

PART THREE
BACK ON THE ROAD

THE WATER WAS NOT CONNECTED, the sink had fallen down inside its wooden housing and the toilet wasn't usable. But the 25-foot RV we borrowed from Joe's grandpa was filled with gas and ready for its journey south.

We chose an RV to cut down on the cost of living but also to transport several rescue dogs to Minnesota upon return. An animal shelter just south of Duluth, Cloquet Friends of Animals, agreed to house up to eight dogs we brought back with us.

There was only one bed in the back of the RV, so we removed the back seats and squeezed in my twin size mattress, which I balanced on top of several dog crates given to us by the Cloquet shelter. Our computers and camera equipment filled the remaining spaces, leaving only a few square feet of room to stand.

The plastic shell of the RV creaked and whined as we merged onto the interstate.

"Creaking Betty," Joe said, fulfilling the important task of naming the vehicle we would be living out of for the next month. Then, he passed me a bag of sunflower seeds from which I filled my cheeks with a handful of shells and let the salt dissolve in my mouth. I watched Duluth get smaller and smaller in the rearview mirror and thought about the tension and heartache leading to that moment. And, for the first time, I felt I was traveling the path

I was meant to travel, one without a clear destination but fueled by a larger purpose. Somewhere in Arkansas we hit our first road bump.

I was driving the speed limit and Joe was in the back of the RV smoking marijuana and listening to a live recording from one of the music festivals he was obsessed with.

This was typical. It reminded me of the time in college when we drove up the north shore of Lake Superior to attend a Trampled by Turtles concert: Joe slammed on the brakes of his 1984 Westphalia van and grabbed his camera to take a picture of a Moose that turned out to be an ornamental, metal cutout.

Joe was diagnosed with epilepsy as a teenager and spent the majority of his boyhood stoned on pharmaceutical drugs that prevented him from seizing. He was introduced to marijuana in college and found it to be a preferable alternative to his seizure medication. I didn't know much about epilepsy, let alone the proper ways to medicate it, so I tried not to put up much of a fight when he lit up a joint. When the smell of weed floated toward the front of the RV, I wasn't surprised.

Then I noticed red and blue flashing lights closing in on us.

"Joe!" I yelled.

Joe!!" I twisted around and yelled again until he took his ear buds out and realized what was happening.

In the rearview mirror I saw a flashlight sweep toward the RV and an officer advancing toward us. I knew I had done nothing wrong but couldn't help feeling like a criminal.

Joe grabbed a can of air freshener and emptied it into the RV. Then he wrapped an American flag bandanna around his head, which is how he always envisioned going to jail for marijuana use. His grand salute to the freethinkers of the 70s, the ones we read about for fun between college semesters.

The officer appeared at the passenger side and tapped on the window with his flashlight. I unbuckled my seat belt and reached over to roll the window down.

"Do you know why I pulled you over?" the officer asked, pointing his light in my eyes. I lifted my hand in front of my face to block the beam of light, then told the officer I was clueless.

"Are you the owner of this vehicle? Where are you headed?" The officer swept his flashlight around the passenger seat and asked me the sort of questions a customs officer might ask at the boarder.

Then, after trying to catch me in a lie, he told me the reason he pulled us over: Our bike rack was covering up the license plate and he couldn't read the numbers. So, out of suspicion and protocol, he pulled us over.

I looked in the rearview mirror, pretending I was trying to see the bike racks, but instead looked at Joe sitting cross-legged on the foldout bed. I felt like a smuggler eyeing the location of his hidden drugs.

When I returned my attention to the officer, his flashlight beamed across my eyes and he explained to me their zero-tolerance policy in the south. He let us off with a written warning and I didn't argue.

INGRID LAW

JOE AND I WERE SITTING IN A BAR AND GRILL in Tuscaloosa hovered over a state map trying to determine the best course of action. A replay of the 2012 BCS National Championship college football game was playing on the corner television.

I was text messaging with Ingrid Law, an animal rescuer who lived near Birmingham and was interested in taking part in our documentary. She said there was a semitruck filled with 80 rescue dogs coming through Birmingham in two hours. The outfit, Rescue Road Trips, was run by Greg Mahle, who drove a truck full of rescue dogs from the South to New England states in the North.

Joe and I rolled up our map, hopped in the RV and drove straight to the Petro station where Rescue Road Trips had scheduled its next stop.

We waited with Ingrid, her neighbor Terry and about 20 other volunteers who showed up to help walk and water the dogs.

Some volunteers were setting up a watering station with a big blue barrel of water and small paper bowls. One of the volunteers made a point of telling me that each dog needs to drink from its own bowl for safety reasons. It was clear to me this wasn't the first time they had prepared to walk and water rescue dogs. Everyone had a role and the whole operation looked routine.

Most of the volunteers were women; in fact, almost all were women. They came straight from work, some with their children and others alone. I wondered what they thought of us, fussing around with camera and audio gear. Looking back at tape from that day, I noticed how beat down and exhausted I was. The southern heat and humidity was not agreeing with my thick, northern blood. Joe set up a camera to record our first interaction with Ingrid and I looked like I was about to tip over.

Ingrid gave us the basics about Greg and his rescue group, how he pulls through the Petro station every other Thursday and Ingrid, along with a few others, spreads the word on Facebook to get as many volunteers as possible.

Greg's cross-country route is 4,200 miles round trip. He averages 80 dogs per trip, which means he saves nearly 2,000 dogs from death row every year. I couldn't imagine what 80 dogs looked like—let alone 2,000—and Ingrid kept repeating that the amount of dogs saved by rescue groups in the South is hardly a drop in the bucket compared to the amount of dogs needing saving.

Joe and I listened to the volunteers and self-proclaimed rescuers banter in a wide circle while we set up our gear. Then Ingrid's phone rang.

"Hello? ... Hey ... What's wrong?" the muscles around Ingrid's mouth twitched nervously, and then she lowered the phone and spoke to the volunteers circled around her. As a photojournalist, I knew we found a great subject to follow. Ingrid was full of energy, and I couldn't wait to hear the news from her phone call. Maybe it would make for good tape.

"Three dogs chained in a vacant house," Ingrid lowered her phone and relayed the information to the group.

"Where? We'll go get 'em," someone said.

"I got my keys, lets go," another woman said as she stepped in front of my camera.

I felt like I was in the locker room before an Alabama State football game; everyone was revved up and ready to go. Suddenly, I felt a jolt of energy.

"Give 'em water and food ASAP, and can you take pictures of 'em and send 'em to me?" Ingrid asked the person on the phone before assuring her that she would figure something out.

This happens all the time: Ingrid gets a call about a problem situation and finds a way to fix it. When she began rescuing animals, it didn't take long for her to gain a reputation in the area as someone who has the capability to get the job done, and now she gets phone calls every day. It's her full time job outside of her full-time job. Rescue isn't something she asked for, it just happened, and now it has grabbed hold of her for good. I couldn't help but think of how easy it would be to ignore those unknown calls and watch Netflix all night, but Ingrid doesn't seem to have that option.

"My phone rings off the hook all day long. I even have people walking into the physical therapy clinic that I manage ... they walk in and they say, 'I need to see Ingrid Law.'

"All the rescuers are swamped, they're just covered up. No matter how much we do, no matter how much time we put into it and how much money we spend, it's not even a drop in the bucket to what's out there, and it's heartbreaking because we work so hard." Ingrid began talking a bit faster and I could tell she was getting worked up.

"We are working ourselves to death trying to fix a problem that other people are responsible for," she said.

It's what we heard over and over from rescuers in the South: *I didn't ask for this, but what am I supposed to do, turn a blind eye?*

If I gleaned anything from my time with Ingrid and other southern rescuers, it's that the idea of relaxing just doesn't register with them; it's not in their deck of cards. They've committed themselves to a cause that they admit is so depressing that they likely won't see the impact of their efforts in their lifetime.

About a year after our film was released, I noticed that Ingrid posted a long, heartfelt message to Facebook, informing her friends and fellow rescuers that she was taking a break from rescue because of the toll it has taken on her. No more than a few weeks later, I saw she was back to posting photos of dogs needing suitable homes.

And, right now, at the very moment I paused from writing this book to scroll my Facebook feed, I saw her post this: "I am desperately looking for somewhere to live where I can take my dogs. They have been staying with my ex, but he says they have to go by the 31st of January. I thought I would be able to bring them where I am currently living, but that's not the case now. I am finding that most people won't allow dogs in rental homes. If you know of anything, please let me know. Out of all the dogs that I have rescued, my own are about to be homeless along with me."

Ingrid says that rescue is a hobby for her; but to an outsider, it's evident that rescue is much more than that: It's who she is, something she was born with. An unshakable characteristic. She would rather be homeless than give up her animals.

When Greg pulled his Rescue Road Trips semitruck into the Petro Station, all of the rescuers cheered, which made me smile because the scene translated well on camera. Before volunteer groups were established along his route, it would take Greg three to four hours to walk and water all of the dogs. Now, with the help of Ingrid and her clan of rescuers stationed outside of Birmingham, Greg is in and out under two hours.

Greg has a second driver help him make the trip. When it's his turn to get sleep, he chooses to roll out a pad in the back of the truck so he can be by the dogs. We only spoke with him for 20 brief minutes, but it was obvious he has a deep love for saving animals. I made a point to ask him why rescue seems to be a predominantly female endeavor in the south.

"I am one of the few, you are right," Greg spoke loud enough to be heard over the rumble of his truck's engine. He said he's been rescuing for seven years and has only come across a handful of male rescuers. He didn't offer insight into why that might be, and I couldn't think of a reason myself, so for the time being, Greg would be classified as an exception to the typical rescue demographic.

Greg hopped in the back of the truck, and Ingrid stood in the doorway where she took dogs from Greg and passed them off to volunteers who were anxious to shower the animals with love.

"This is Whoopy. He's a tripod," Ingrid yelled out to the volunteer who was next in line to grab a dog.

"Little Boy," Ingird grinned and handed off a young black lab to an oversized volunteer, which made me grin too.

"Scruffy," Ingrid picked up the next dog and it started peeing toward my camera.

"He had to go!" An elderly volunteer spoke to the dog in a sweet, motherly tone.

Once all of the dogs were out of the truck, I sat down on a curb next to Terri Richards, a middle-aged volunteer with dyed blonde hair who was rubbing down a dog.

"I wish I could get the lottery," she said. "There would never be another stray, there would never be another hungry dog."

The idea of money raised an important question: Can more funding fix a problem that seems to be so culturally ingrained?

It was a question we asked Brenda Lafontaine, a friend of Ingrid who owns a successful parking business and spent over six figures on animal rescue the previous year.

"You mentioned before that you put in $100,000 toward animal rescue but that it really doesn't make a difference. Can you talk about that?" I asked Brenda.

"I've not said publicly what that number was before, but I've decided to do it now because it's very clear that money alone is not going to solve the problem," Brenda said. "There are just so many dogs; it's such a huge problem. $100,000 didn't make a dent, and I don't know if a million would, so it becomes a matter of how can we spend that money in a way that will be meaningful for future dogs as well as the ones we are trying to save today."

Full disclosure: Brenda was the main financial backer of our documentary film, "Roots of Rescue," albeit the budget for our film was very small compared to most. Still, we were extremely grateful that Brenda saw the importance of storytelling as a means to help save more companion animals. Someone, and I wish I could remember who, told me that you use whatever skill or asset you have to assist in the fight. Rescue can be hands on, it can be a financial contribution, or in my case, a story. You do what you do. But no matter the approach, the problem seemed to simmer on, which begged the question: What is the best approach, and how can the fight to end animal cruelty and overpopulation be better targeted?

"If I knew the answer, I would be yelling it from rooftops, but it boils down, I think, to two things and that is education and legislation," Brenda said.

Maybe that was the source of Ingrid's tension and anger, the not knowing how to efficiently fix a larger cultural problem. Just as Brenda knows that no amount of money will bring an end to the suffering of companion animals, Ingrid knows that rescuing 50 to 100 dogs each year is only a drop in the bucket, but she does it anyway and I wanted to know why. I wanted to see what she sees so maybe I could better understand why these women continue swimming against a current that is just too strong and pulls them into eddies, tossing them in circles.

We met Ingrid at the same Petro Station the next day. She agreed, with little convincing, to let us poke further into her life as an animal rescuer.

She pulled up in her silver Volkswagen bug and told us about a possible dog-fighting ring in a nice suburban neighborhood. This information was acquired from a veterinarian who Ingrid referred to as Dr. H. I was excited that we finally had an ear to the ground in the world of dog fighting, a world we had yet to fully explore.

Dr. H received an anonymous phone call reporting animal fighting in that person's neighborhood. There is a reason the caller was anonymous and a reason Dr. H will never be anything more than Dr. H ... they fear for their lives. So I asked Ingrid why she doesn't share that same fear.

"Well, I hope I don't get shot one day, but it's a risk I'm willing to take," Ingrid said. "If there was a dog fighter here in my presence, we're on my property, he better move fast," Ingrid looked back and forth between Joe and I and let out a laugh that made me realize she was telling the truth. Given the opportunity, she would snap and as she told us, "It wouldn't be good."

Joe and I certainly didn't have the same gut as Ingrid, so it was likely our ignorance that led us to hop in her car and drive to the site where potential dog fighting was taking place.

We drove slowly down a road, reading house numbers. The 1985 rock song, 'Lovin' Every Minute of It' played through the radio, providing us with a little motivational energy, enough to cloud our judgment.

Ingrid showed me her black revolver, which initially made me feel safer but eventually made me realize the threat of danger must be real enough for her to carry such a weapon. I moved nervously in my seat and refocused my attention to my camera. It's something I was used to doing; if I felt uncomfortable in a situation, I would look at the scene through my camera, which helped me detach from the reality of what was happening. I could think in numbers of shutter speed and aperture instead of feeling the emotions of fear and discomfort.

My camera was balanced on a shoulder mount with a 200mm lens, the same lens my father used to take pictures of me playing hockey as a kid. I purposefully framed a crack in Ingrid's windshield in the shot to give the video a more rustic feel, but when we finally made it to the dog-fighting house, I realized there was nothing rustic or grungy about the scene.

The house was solid brick. Two pillars flanking the driveway, both topped with giant stone lions, stood firm and menacing. A huge privacy fence stretched back into the woods and skirted the perimeter at the back of the property.

"They said it was a nice house, and that is a nice house," Ingrid said, affirming we had found the right place.

There was no sign that anybody was home, so after we passed the house Ingrid made a U-turn, drove back and crept down the driveway.

I could feel my palms start to sweat and my eyes widen like some sort of small animal prey. Ingrid turned the music down slightly.

Turn that dial all the way
Shoot me like a rocket into space
Lovin' every minute of it
Lovin' every minute of it

I wondered how Ingrid could be so calm and reserved while I was squirming in my 24-year-old, fit body.

"There's a dog over there," Ingrid said, and I swung my camera around toward a pit bull chained up next to a strange looking wooden box.

"What's this, drive up," Joe said, pointing to a dog hide hanging over the fence.

I adjusted a ring on my lens and brought the hide into clear focus.

Fuck, I thought. There are some scenes that you can't detach yourself from by viewing them through a camera lens, and this was one of them.

"I think probably more evidence is going to be behind this fence, where that pavilion is back there," Ingrid decided to pull out of the driveway and park down the road so we could go in on foot and investigate further. Investigating, however, is too strong of a word. Snooping and trespassing are more accurate.

We walked the tree line at the edge of the property, following Ingrid. When we were hidden behind a shrub, Ingrid stopped and lowered her sunglasses to get a better look at the backyard.

"There's another dog," she said, and it must have seen us too because it began growling, which roused the rest of the dogs and set the backyard off into a chorus of clinking chains and deep, drool-shaking barking.

When we reached the front corner of the privacy fence, we peeked through the wooden slats. There was a shed and cluster of trees blocking our view, so we walked toward the back of the property.

Ingrid climbed the fence and peeked over.

"One, two, three, four, five, six, seven ... there's seven dogs," Ingrid pointed out how all of the dogs were attached to heavy log chains, even though they were well confined in a spacious backyard.

"So what do you suspect," I asked.

"Something's going on here," she said with a short laugh.

I changed my position to get a better shot of Ingrid looking over the fence.

"Eight, I just saw another dog. There's one in the very back corner," Ingrid said.

All of the dogs were pit bulls, none were neutered and all seemed to be well fed, which Ingrid said made sense if they were used for fighting. She stepped down from the fence, looking upset.

"It's heartbreaking," she said, pausing to peek through the slats. "You see how nice this house is, too? This goes to show you that this goes on, it's not just in the city, in the projects, I mean this is a nice house and its going on right here. This is 10 minutes from where I live, 10 minutes from my neighborhood, right down the street from an elementary school."

Her reaction was familiar and reminded me of the time a sex offender moved into the neighborhood where my high school girlfriend lived. I was shocked, upset, frustrated and fearful for her safety.

Growing up, I felt like danger was real, but never imminent. I imagine Ingrid held the same thought concerning dog abuse: It would never occur close to where she lived. It happens, but it happens somewhere else, by someone you don't know and don't understand. But that's just something we tell ourselves to feel safe. The reality is completely contradictory. And there we were, trampling through its backyard.

We followed Ingrid as she walked back down the length of the property and onto the driveway where the dog hide was draped over the top of the fence. Next to it was a metal burn barrel.

"It just makes me sick," Ingrid said. "I'm going back here."

Ingrid walked into the fenced in backyard where the dogs were chained. We noticed security cameras under the eaves of the house and I started to feel extremely uncomfortable and exposed. I let my camera roll but was no longer paying attention to it; I had my head on a swivel and began thinking of worst-case scenarios.

Maybe somebody is home.

If I have to run, I will throw my camera over the fence first.

What if we get shot at?

Fuck.

Fuck.

Fuck.

I was paranoid.

"One, two, three, four, five, six, seven, eight, nine, ten," Ingrid counted two more dogs she had missed before. "There's ten," she said.

"I'm going to make some phone calls and figure out the best route to take.

"We know they're fighting dogs here, so a dog died and for some reason someone skinned the dog and left the hide on the fence. I don't know what that's about," Ingrid said.

I didn't know either; in fact, I could hardly believe the hide belonged to a dog. I kept thinking it must be some other animal. It's easy to second guess yourself when what you see is so sadistic and you can't come up with a reason why.

Why? You ask yourself.

Why?

WHY?

You want so badly to understand but you can't find either end of a line of logic, whatsoever, none. No rational explanation exists. All you're left with is frustration and anger.

I was beginning to understand why Ingrid twitched when she received that phone call in the Petro Station parking lot and why she sounded so serious when she said "it wouldn't be good" if a dog fighter crossed her path. She was drowning in anger.

My next assumption was that we could do something about the situation. We knew where the dog-fighters lived and had seen the evidence. Now we could have them locked up.

As it turned out, there was more to the game.

Ingrid drove us back to the Petro Station and we tossed around ideas for our next step. She decided to call the state chair of AVRAL, Alabama Voters for Responsible Animal Legislation, Rhonda Parker, for advice.

Joe and I tapped a line into her phone so we could hear both ends of the conversation.

"We counted 10 pit bulls in the very back of the yard inside of a privacy fence," Ingrid relayed all we had seen, including the only female dog that was separated from the rest of the dogs and chained up next to that strange-looking box. When Ingrid described the box, Rhonda knew exactly what it was.

"It's a rape stand," she said, referring to the method of forced breeding.

I wanted to puke.

"A dog has been skinned and the hide is laying over the fence," Ingrid added.

I made a quick adjustment in my video frame for dramatic appeal.

"What?" Rhonda's voice peeked the meter on our audio recorder.

"Right next to that is like a 55-gallon drum with ashes in it," Ingrid paused. "Imagine what that was."

"Oh shit," I could sense Rhonda's heart bottom out in her chest after imagining what we were all imaging: a companion animal ruthlessly reduced to ashes in a barrel by dog fighters who likely can't see the difference between burning a dog and burning a pile of brush in the fall.

Again, I wanted to puke.

Rhonda told us about a group out of Atlanta, Georgia, headed by an ex-marine and a squad of retired policemen that specializes in investigating dog fighting.

"They make a lot of busts," she said.

I lost myself in a daydream of a well-armed outfit of men moving in on the house, busting down doors and wheeling the dog fighters away, dragging them by their hair so they kicked and screamed like the little punk children they are. I knew that vision probably didn't fit the reality of how the Atlanta group worked.

Unfortunately, the Atlanta outfit wasn't able to investigate that property during the time Joe and I allotted to be in Alabama.

Fuck, I thought.

I wanted to film a success. I wanted to see the faces of dog fighters and study them for signs of remorse. Like Ingrid, I wanted nothing more than closure, for the dust to settle.

We returned to Ingrid's house feeling defeated. Ingrid came outside with a watermelon that we fed to her pig. Yes, she has a pig, and it's wildly fun to watch it snort away the core of a watery fruit.

When the pig was finished, we wandered over to Ingrid's neighbors house and sat around her pool. The sun was down, and the day seemed like it had reached an end, but Ingrid was revved up and couldn't shake the thought of a dog-fighting ring in a five-mile radius of her home. I have never been to war, I have no Afghanistan story, but imagine this is what it felt like when the enemy was advancing on you and you felt the need to flex some muscle.

We assumed a dead dog hide was evidence enough to bring to the authorities, but Ingrid informed us that we had to catch them in the act. We had to show them fighting; the remnants of war were not enough. That's what the Atlanta group was good at, but unfortunately, we didn't have them.

We weren't recording our conversation on camera that night, so I don't have direct quotes, but I can assure you that Ingrid's comments were punctuated with expletives. She was pissed and decided to call her neighbor who was a cop.

Joe lit up a cigar and fetched us more beer, and before long, the cop neighbor emerged from the darkness. I stood up to shake his hand, Joe did the same, then Ingrid told him all about what we had seen and asked if he could check it out with us. As expected, the cop echoed what we already knew ... there was little he could do unless he had proof of dog fighting.

Go get it, I thought, hoping he could somehow read my mind. But I didn't dare say it out loud.

Ingrid, however, was less conservative. She told him she wanted to return to the house and throw a brick through the window; either that, or sneak back into the fenced-in yard and cut all of the dogs loose. To this, the cop neighbor laughed quietly and advised Ingrid to stay put and try not to think about it too much, which bothered me, not because I wanted to see Ingrid throw a brick through a dog fighter's window, but because the cop was able to laugh it off so easily. Isn't it his job to worry about things like that? Where there is dog fighting, there is drug use and scores of other criminal acts. Isn't that his business? Does he not care that these things are happening in the vicinity of an elementary school?

No. Supposedly it's Ingrid's business. And because she couldn't wait for a security group from Atlanta to ride in on their white horses, she told Terry to pull her SUV around so we could return to the house with video cameras and try to catch the bastards in the act ourselves.

Ingrid reached that threshold of stress that begged for a cigarette, so she rolled the window down and lit one up.

Another piece of information Dr. H provided was that the people fighting the dogs were black. I'm bringing this up because I feel an obligation to include what Ingrid's neighbor said when we got in the car.

"You have to understand," she said. "The black down here are different from the North, they're very dangerous down here."

Her comment made me cringe. I'm not saying she doesn't have justifiable evidence to back it up, but it made me realize that the South is still segregated; there are still "black neighborhoods" and "white neighborhoods." That comment was a generalization, one that I couldn't help but think aids in the suppression of black people in the South and possibly perpetuates the culture of animal cruelty.

It reminded me of what my grandpa told me about the people in the south. He told me I should think twice before going on the trip and messing with dog fighters because the people from the south that he knew from his military training are a different breed.

"They're mean," he told me.

I shrugged him off then, but his comment hung in the air with me whenever I toed the line of danger.

"Supposed to be 96 tomorrow," Ingrid said, breaking the silence and putting an end to my daydream. And just like that, the race conversation was over. It bothered me that the majority of the abuse situations we came across involved black perpetrators, and I wanted so badly for the next criminal to be white so our film wouldn't come across as racist. But maybe race shouldn't matter. After all, abuse is abuse.

End of digression.

I leaned over to see the shot Joe had framed of Ingrid's hand holding her cigarette near the window. Its ember tip flickered and oscillated with heat.

Nice shot, I thought.

A financial commercial marketed to senior citizens played through the radio, and for a moment, I almost forgot where we were going.

As we pulled up to the house, Ingrid motioned for her neighbor to slow the car. There were lights on in the house and a truck parked outside; other than that, nothing seemed out of the ordinary.

It made me wonder how often these people fight their dogs. Is there a schedule posted on some obscure, fronted website? It would take dumb luck to happen upon the action and even more dumb luck to get close enough to film it undetected.

We traveled along the road behind the house to see if we missed something, thinking maybe they keep the action further back in the woods, but we saw nothing. Crickets chirped in the ditches and an old Rottweiler's chain clinked as it raised its head to learn why a car was slowing down on the street.

The whole thing was depressing: two middle-aged women with two young journalists in tow creeping around a dog-fighting operation. What the hell were we doing? What would we actually do if illegal activity were taking place? It was crazy to think we could actually do any good.

But if not us, then who?

Ingrid sucked on her cigarette and we drove back to her house where Joe and I passed out in the RV next to the pig's kennel.

ON THE FRONTLINE

WE HAD TO KEEP MOVING. We were on a limited time frame and needed to meet and interview as many animal rescuers as we could to get the big picture of animal rescue and rescuers alike.

I thumbed over the next name in my reporter's notebook, Tina Watson, and made plans to meet with her that afternoon at her home in Cottondale, just East of Tuscaloosa.

It was our third day bouncing from city to city, and the affects of road life started to show. We had yet to shower, aside from the occasional wind shower that consisted of hanging our heads out the RV windows while rumbling down Interstate 20 between Birmingham and Tuscaloosa. I chose to wear the same shirt every day because of its convenient zip-up pockets that carried extra camera batteries and memory cards. It was the same shirt I wore to a wedding earlier that year and that Joe said made me look like Ace Ventura. The armpits started to yellow and gather layers of old deodorant.

We missed Tina's house at first pass, which was tucked behind a nonresidential building. I was sweating my ass off and trying to gauge how long it would take for my body to acclimate to southern temperatures. I took several gulps from a gallon jug of water before jumping out into the swelter of Alabama's high humidity.

Tina met us at the gate in front of her house where two of her dogs were already jumping to greet us. She shooed them away so we could squeeze through and follow her inside where it was dark and cool.

Watson, Tina's black pit mix ran down from an L-shaped sofa taking up the majority of her living room and pushed its nose against my leg. Tina's more stalky, brindle pit bull, Girlfriend, stood firmly in the middle of the room barking at the unfamiliar visitors carrying strange gear into the house. It took a moment for Tina to calm her dogs before we could begin a conversation.

She walked us through her kitchen where several dogs were crated and waiting to be adopted. Tina recommended we take one with us, and we told her we would on our way back to Minnesota.

Like all of the southern women we met, Tina's "hobby" of rescue began organically. She started just more than a year prior to us meeting by rescuing her dog, Girlfriend along with Girlfriend's litter of 10 puppies from an abandoned home. Like Ingrid, Tina gained a reputation as someone to call about strays and abandoned animals. Do it once, better be prepared to do it again.

Her first year as a self-proclaimed animal rescuer she saved 60 dogs, which seemed like a lot, but Tina said all she does is drive to abandoned homes where, more often than not, she finds neglected dogs chained and left to rot. They are the dogs occupying crates in Tina's kitchen. Some have bandages over old wounds.

"Even when you try to take a break, there's no break," Tina said.

Because her house was busy with animals, we decided to hop in her SUV and interview her as she followed up on a potential rescue situation. I noticed her license plate read "4PITS," so I crouched to get a shot of it before climbing in the vehicle. We thanked Tina for taking time out of her day to let us film her: She was working 60 hours a week but managed to carve time out of her afternoon.

"We're going to ride to the west side of Tuscaloosa, Alabama, and try to see a mother pit and three puppies that are running loose in a yard," Tina said, explaining that a man contacted her about his neighbor's dog that just had puppies. That neighbor said the owner didn't want the puppies and was looking to get rid of them.

In theory, it should be an easy rescue.

"This is the first time I will ever actually speak to an owner face to face at their home about their dogs, because I've never done that," Tina smiled. "We're going to see if the family will release the puppies to us and also allow us to either spay the mother dog or release the mother dog to us as well."

We hit a stoplight and a dark SUV pulled up next to us. A couple of rough-looking guys were curious about the camera I had pointed at Tina and I could see one of them mouth the words *what the fuck*. They matched our speed as we continued down the highway, so I zoomed in on Tina to get a tighter image, attempting to crop the gawkers out of the shot, or at least blur them slightly.

"If they don't let you take these puppies, what do you think will happen?" I asked.

"They will get into the hands of the wrong people. They will be used as bait dogs or be trained as fighting dogs. Being that they're lab mix, I think that someone would want to use them as bait dogs versus pit bull-fighting dogs because usually it's the ones that they call pure breeds with the best bloodlines that they want to fight." Tina was rubbing her arm, which told me she was nervous to be on camera.

"They could be tortured by children," she added as another possible destiny for the newly born pups, which caught my attention more than the alternatives because it signified how deeply engrained the culture of animal cruelty was.

Tortured by children? I thought in disbelief.

Immediately, I called up memories of my own upbringing and association with childhood pets and felt sad that not everyone is granted the same education on how to properly treat an animal. I specifically recalled a time when I was playing with our family pet and began tossing toys at her. I was getting out of control and tossing the toys pretty hard. My father caught me and gave me an earful on how what I was doing was borderline abusive. My heart sank and I never did it again.

We drove in silence for a few moments and I imagined both Tina and Joe were calling up memories of their own, the ones that make you stop and ask yourself what makes you different.

We finally made it to the house with the pit bull and puppies, and the owner was sitting on his porch enjoying a smoke. The three of us climbed out of the SUV and walked up to him, cameras rolling and boom microphone hovering overhead like a giant blimp at a sports game.

Tina introduced herself and asked if the man was the owner of the red nose pit bull. He said he was. Then Tina asked if he was still looking to get rid of the puppies. He nodded and said "Probably, yeah."

All right, cool, this shouldn't take long.

"My name is Tina Watson, I do animal rescue," Tina offered him a handshake and the man flipped his cigarette back into his mouth to free his shaking hand.

Tina asked him if the puppies were in the yard and if she could see them. Then she asked if he wanted her to spay the mother pit bull.

The man squirmed uncomfortably on the porch bench and stared off between Tina, Joe and myself, visibly upset by her question.

"No, I don't want her spayed," he said, but his body language read something like, *Fuck you, lady.*

"Why not?" Tina pressed, asking how many puppies the mother dog had.

"She had about nine." The man leaned back, and I zoomed the camera lens out for a wider shot.

"Where are the other six?" Tina asked.

"Some of them died," the man responded, far too calmly given the subject.

Tina asked to see the remaining three puppies and told the man that she rescues, vets and adopts out animals. They would be in good hands, she assured him.

"Well I'm just getting up, so you done caught me at a bad time, so I ain't moving no dogs right now." The man's sentence was slurred together.

Tina asked the man if he would at least reconsider letting her spay the mother dog, to which he responded he might take her to Joplin, Missouri, which basically meant that he wanted the option to breed her so he could sell the puppies as bait dogs to fighters.

Tina pressed further until the man made it clear he didn't want the dog spayed, so she left him her card and walked quickly back to the SUV with her head down and brow furrowed.

"I don't understand," she said.

"What's your assumption?" I asked. "Why do you think he doesn't want to spay his dog?"

"Because if she's a purebred red nose like he said she is, then he can breed her," Tina said, referring to the value of a purebred pit bull to dogfighters. "Apparently he knows somebody in Joplin, because he spit out Joplin as fast as he could."

The mother dog, to its owner, was considered a commodity. It stays roped to a tree in the backyard and when the time is right, will be sold for its potential to breed expensive offspring. That dog is no different than a rusted car sitting in a front yard with a For Sale sign slapped to the windshield. So when the neighbor heard the owner wanted to get rid of the puppies, he likely didn't realize the man was looking for a bidder, not a rescuer. Nevertheless, word got around to Tina and her first face-to-face interaction with a dog owner was chalked up as a failure, or at least a learning experience.

"We tried and I'll still follow up on it," Tina said.

Her plan was to return without us in hopes the absence of cameras would make the man feel more comfortable. I hoped she was right, but even Tina knew it was likely a lost cause.

We pulled back up to Tina's house and filmed some "promo" style material of Tina holding her pit bulls on leash. Joe tried to record audio of Watson panting, but every time the microphone got close, Watson tried to bite the fuzzy wind filter.

I fetched my jug of water from the RV and took a long drink before following Tina back inside her air-conditioned home. We asked her if there were any other potential rescue trips we could accompany her on and she told us about a report of a man who trains his fighting dog in his backyard most nights around 10 p.m. by encouraging it to attack a smaller bait dog. The neighbor witnessed it from the privacy of his rear window and said the man puts his foot down on the dog's neck, holding it down against the dirt and against its will, while the pit bull viciously attacked.

Ruthless, I thought while I replayed the situation in my head, trying to understand the motivation behind such an act.

The bait dog, Tina said, probably wouldn't live much longer, so she recommended we sneak around the property and try to get footage of it, and if possible, try to rescue—steal—the bait dog. It's something we debated as we drove back toward Birmingham, where we got a campsite at Oak Mountain State Park.

I scraped away at a package of tuna with my camping spork and washed it down with a bottle of Joe's homebrewed beer as we set up camp. We carried with us food that wouldn't spoil and ate from cheap fast food joints and gas stations.

So ... tuna and beer. Down the hatch.

Oak Mountain is Alabama's largest state park and spans nearly 10,000 acres. Visitors can enjoy its 50 miles of hiking and biking trails, shoreline fishing, and sandy beeches. Joe and I stripped down to our shorts and rode our bikes to the nearest beach where the water was piss warm and didn't feel nearly as refreshing as anticipated, so we retreated back to the RV and tore into the 30 pack of Hamm's beer Joe's uncle gave to us as a parting gift and sustenance for the long road.

I was eager to clean myself, so I hooked a hose up to the water spigot and clamped it to one of our light stands, creating a backwoods, hillbilly shower. I lathered on a layer of soap and rinsed off in the open air while Joe huddled away in the RV smoking a joint.

We spent some time considering what we would do the next day. Not having a plan irritated me and made me feel like we were an unprofessional documentary film crew, which in reality, was probably true.

I snapped back the top on another Hamm's and took a seat at the picnic table while Joe fired up his camp stove to cook rice, onions and whatever else we had in the RV—a camping mash of sorts.

Again, I thumbed through my reporters notebook trying to decide who to speak with next, all the while thinking of Tina's recommendation to try to rescue a bait dog that would likely die soon if nobody did anything.

As a reporter, the idea of injecting ourselves into the story and becoming animal rescuers seemed like a big red flag.

Don't do it, I thought. *Maintain objectivity and separation from the subjects and issues at hand.*

Being fresh out of journalism school, I felt the need to go by the book, but as I witnessed over and over again, none of the rescuers asked for the rescue life, it simply showed up on their doorstep, or their moral compass pointed them in the direction of rescue. I knew I was being lured in the same direction and there was little I could do to fight it, and so as journalists sometimes do, I spun it, deciding that walking in a rescuer's shoes might help me better understand what their life is truly like. Gonzo journalism.

Before returning to Cottondale to check up on the bait dog situation, we decided to spend our fourth day visiting my college advisor, Adam, and his wife, Kim. Since they set us off on our adventure, we decided we needed to interview them for the documentary.

We gassed up, bought a Crimson Tide window flag in attempts to fit in with the masses, and bounced back down the road. When I was finished working the shells off a wad of sunflower seeds in my mouth, I rolled down the window to dispose of them, which sent the newly purchased Crimson Tide flag flying behind us. Our attempt to fit in lasted the amount of time it took me to deshell a handful of seeds.

When we entered Adam and Kim's house, Adam's dog, Dudley, nudged up against us. I patted him down while the four of us caught up on our progress filming. Then we sat Kim down for an official interview.

Kim moved to Alabama years ago from the North and said she began to notice all of the things Joe and I noticed regarding animals in the South: overpopulation, dogs chained and emaciated, dead dogs along highways and backcountry roads, and even dog fighting. She wanted to learn more, so she began working with rescue groups. As a musician, Kim found a unique way to advocate for southern companion animals.

"I've tried to, with my music, create a platform where I can raise awareness and talk about these issues on a more global level." Kim was seated on a piano bench next to a copy of her album, so I panned my camera to reveal it. Her band, Berteal, comprises Kim and her brother, and they donate album sales to animal welfare causes.

"I started writing songs about these issues, and Berteal performs at different places I kind of use it as my soap box," she said. "I just feel like that is my mission. I want to use every little ounce of talent or ability God has given me for this topic."

One of Kim's most popular songs, 'On the Frontline,' echoes the heartache felt by rescuers who, through no choice of their own, find themselves on the frontline fighting against animal abuse and neglect.

My heart feels like a dog chained to a tree
Victim of neglect and cruelty
And so it goes

And so it goes

I look around and everywhere I see
Signs of pain and inhumanity
And so it goes
And so it goes

Meet me on the frontline of
This war to save the helpless ones
Come and fight by my side
On the frontline
On the frontline

"You break your body down, you wreck your finances, you wreck your relationships, you spend every hour, every minute you can and you still feel like it's not a drop in the bucket," Kim paused and looked down at the floor. "It's so discouraging, I don't know the answer. I mean you'll hear people say, 'Oh, it's advocacy,' 'Oh, it's awareness,' 'Oh it's education,' 'Oh, it's spay and neuter.' It is, it's all those things, but it has to be enough people doing those things."

The desperation in Kim's voice, I imagined, mirrored the desperation that bait dog in Cottondale was feeling. And in that moment, I was successfully recruited as an animal rescuer: I would return to Cottondale and at least attempt to do something.

Stand up and do something, I repeated to myself what Kim was trying to convey in her music.

Meet me on the frontline of
This war to save the helpless ones
Come and fight by my side
On the frontline
On the frontline

The following night, our fifth night on the road, Joe and I parked the RV in a church parking lot a few blocks from where the dog fighter was reported to have been training his fighting dog.

Joe took a pull of whiskey and I took a pull of gin.

Joe pocketed a knife and handed me brass knuckles ... just in case.

We said a few words into the camera about what we were about to do before stepping quietly outside the RV and walking down Mary Lee Avenue, where we had no idea what would happen.

I stopped to get a shot of the street sign and Joe motioned for me to keep walking so he could film my shadow stretching across the blacktop.

My senses were heightened as I isolated every sound or change in light, dissecting the environment for potential danger. A mass of crickets could be heard rubbing their legs in a chirping symphony, which masked the sound of our footsteps. A car missing its muffler huffed its way down a distant road and petered out.

"There's definitely a bait dog back there getting the shit ripped out of it. Do you hear yelping?" Joe whispered.

"Yeah," I said and felt my heart stop and skin tingle.

"Let's bust this motherfucker wide open and then run," Joe said excitedly.

Listening back on tape from that night is confusing because I don't remember Joe saying any of this, yet there it is, recorded and registering with me for the first time through my computer speakers. I must have been blocking everything out, curling up inside with fear, numb as the bait dog we were searching for.

We reached the end of Mary Lee Avenue and turned down a gravel alleyway where we discussed what to do next. There were dogs everywhere; one even followed us down the road until we were well clear of its property. We had no idea which house to be looking at or which animal noise to focus on. I felt like I was underwater, in vertigo.

A foot trail ventured off into the woods at the end of the road, which we assumed might lead to a pit bull-fighting ring. I imagined walking its dark corridor and stumbling upon a group of thugs huddled around two animals digging their teeth into each other. Just then, the steel screeching of a train cut sharply down the alley. I was relieved to have cover-up noise while Joe and I considered our options.

We tried to peak through backyards to catch a glimpse of the bait dog but were interrupted by a car with cheap rims that turned down Mary Lee and rounded the corner of the alley, it's headlights illuminating us like deer on a county road.

Joe and I held our cameras down at our sides as the car passed and came to a slow roll at the end of the alley. We stopped walking as a truck followed closely behind, passing us slowly. I was blinded by its headlights and couldn't make out its occupants. The first car stopped at the end of the alley. Something wasn't right.

So we ran.

We ran across Mary Lee, hopped a fence and came out in the church parking lot where the RV was parked. I swung my body inside and flipped on my camera.

"If you're going to drive through the hood, I recommend having a fast getaway vehicle … like this V6 RV," I joked, relieved to be safe inside the vehicle.

Joe flicked the bobbly Jesus figurine on the dashboard as we pulled back onto Interstate 20 to drive back to Oak Mountain. I watched it sway back and forth as if praying for us.

How does Bonnie do this every day? I thought. *And Ingrid and Tina?*

I felt pathetic. Like I failed that bait dog. I had no idea what it takes to partake in animal rescue and enact a down-south style of justice. To "bust this motherfucker open and run."

SONYA SMITH

SONYA SMITH LOOKS LIKE SHE SPENDS MOST OF HER TIME SIPPING cocktails with her girlfriends at country clubs and swanky hotel restaurants. She's in great shape and wears a sundress and bug-like sunglasses. Her skin is perfect and lips glossed. Think Southern Bell, and you'll see Sonya: soft spoken, polite and attractive. But she's not afraid to get her dress dirty.

We followed her into a dilapidated, abandoned home and tiptoed around a giant hole in the middle of what used to be a living room. The floor rotted away and fell through to the crawl space below.

"Hello?" Sonya's sweet voice echoed through the house like a savior angel.

We stepped over a mattress and Sonya pointed to a pile of dog food that she had left at the house before.

"I think sometimes a human eats it actually," she said, before returning her attention to the hole in the middle of the room where a stray dog might be curled up. She made a clicking noise and called "Here baby, baby, baby," like a mother trying to get her child to take its first steps.

"Any babies in here today?" she called out again, crouching near the hole in her sundress.

Sonya is the director of Two by Two Animal Rescue in Helena, Alabama, a suburb of Birmingham. She has a law degree but decided to dedicate her time to animal rescue instead of pursuing a career in law.

"About 11 years ago I moved to the area, and I kept noticing the same strays in old town Helena and they were dodging traffic and they were emaciated and you could tell some of them just had puppies," Sonya said.

Every chance she got, Sonya stopped to feed and water strays. She wanted to bring them home with her but didn't have the space, so she decided to talk to the mayor about the land the city appropriated for animal control. It had six small kennels and wasn't being used.

"I wouldn't mind running around doing the leg work of catching the strays if he wouldn't mind me using the land that they had appropriated for an animal shelter," Sonya explained. "He just handed me the key and said 'knock yourself out.'"

We were sitting in Sonya's kitchen asking her how she got started in rescue. It seemed curious to us that she chose to give up on a potentially lucrative career in law. Just behind her, I noticed a colorful piece of paper taped to the microwave door that read, "Go Boldly to God." Her house was full of similar reminders of faith.

"I love being a southern girl, my mom raised me to be a Southern Bell, and there's a lot that I'm proud of. But when it comes to the treatment of animals—and I would really even have to add children—in the South, it makes me drop my head, it really does." Sonya looked down at her colorful running shoes, considering carefully what to say next. "We honor a lot of things in the South that are superficial. We're football fanatics and families will split over a football team, but the real issues are how we treat the least, and there is a lack of education and a lack of just compassion." Sonya looked at me with her caramel eyes, and it was impossible for me not to feel something in that moment. "There's a lot of suffering, not just out of ignorance but there is intentional suffering."

The Bible passages and reminders of faith posted around Sonya's house made me nervous. Everywhere I looked, I was confronted by another colorful note telling me to be a good person, which, at 24, was haunting. My life mistakes were only beginning, and I felt too cynical to remind myself of my own flaws. But for Sonya, they were reminders to keep faith and not loose focus.

Saving one dog won't change the world, she said, but it will change the world of that dog.

"Sometimes it feels like a fight that's too big for the battle, but we just have to trust that we're doing the right things, that we are honoring God's creatures, and that he is going to bless us for blessing them," Sonya said.

Helena, which has a population under 20,000, has a much higher median household income than Alabama's state average and was ranked in Money Magazine's 2007 list of "Best Places to Live: Top 100." Sonya said the mayor told her Two by Two Animal Rescue was a big reason Helena made that list.

"We're pretty sure we're the only No Kill animal control in the country. There are No Kill rescues, but for an animal control to be No Kill, that's far and in-between." Sonya said. "That is able to exist because of the partnership the city has with a nonprofit with a No Kill philosophy."

I couldn't believe what I was hearing. It seemed everywhere we went, rescuers were working their asses off with little results, while just miles away, this charming Southern Bell was able to fix the stray animal problem in her city by collaborating with local officials and community members.

It's safe to say that the animal abuse is less prevalent in Helena than in Greene County, but that doesn't mean there isn't a lesson to be learned from the way Sonya went about making a difference.

"Other cities and counties and other rescues have really inquired as to our model of what we do," she said. "For the smaller cities in the rural areas, this is very doable, where the city has already appropriated property and some fencing or something to house the dogs. When you have a low number of dogs that are on the intake, it's very doable to raise the money for the veterinarian fees so that it does not automatically come out of the city's budget, and that is why we are so successful."

The formula seemed foolproof to me: low animal intake + helpful city officials + cooperative community members = an animal-friendly, healthy environment. The same formula could be used to solve any number of problems in a community, but the reality is, that formula is hard to put together.

In a way, what is happening in Helena is the answer, but it's also the outlier. Each of the communities we visited prior to Helena seemed to be missing one or several ingredients in the formula. Low animal intake? That wasn't the case anywhere we visited outside Helena. Helpful city officials? Maybe. Here or there. Cooperative community member? Sometimes. In some places.

Adoption fees, grants and private donations fund Two by Two Animal Rescue. Through their many years of work and credibility, people have even chosen to leave them estates in their wills.

"We have been very blessed and we've really seen that if you do a good job and you're consistent, and you do the best you can with what you have, and you're a good steward with the money, the community will jump behind you and support you," Sonya said.

On a typical day, Sonya's rescue dog, Eli, rides shotgun. Eli has a thyroid problem that prevents his fur from fully growing in. At first glance, he looks mangy. Sonya opened the hatch of her SUV, rubbed Eli under the snout and bumped noses with him.

"Eli the sailor man," she sang and flirted with her dog.

I took Eli's place riding shotgun as Sonya guided us on her daily routine.

"I just ride certain streets every day just keeping my eyes peeled for what's going on. I know all the dogs in the area, so it helps just to keep track of what's going on: who's pregnant, who's chained up, which owners will let you take 'em to the vet, which owners don't like you messing," Sonya said, looking left, then right, scanning each property for signs of stray animals or cruelty situations.

It's important to note that even though Sonya has made a huge difference in her community, it's still an ongoing battle.

"Especially in this area, a dog is just a dog, so they're treated like that," she said. "There's a lot that need my help."

Sonya stopped the vehicle and pointed out a utility shed where two homeless brothers sometimes take shelter.

"From time to time they'll let a puppy or a dog sort of hang out with them, and I'm on the lookout for this little brindle male dog that I caught and then he got away from me, so I'm hoping he set up refuge back here." Sonya hopped out, taking a bag of dog treats with her. "They know me so they don't mind me coming to check."

Sonya made clicking noises with her tongue and roof of her mouth and called out "Here pumpkin! Here pumpkin!" She rapped on the shed door but nobody answered so we walked back the SUV and continued our search for the brindle dog. I thought it was daring of Sonya to be walking blindly into situations where she could be faced with danger.

"I've been told I'm very naive and foolish, but I've never really had a reason to be scared," Sonya said. "I'll be honest, when I first started rescue, I just got real angry and you just want to strangle 'em. You learn that they are a product of their environment, they are a product of lack of education, and if you just extend some kindness back, the walls will come down."

We drove to what was considered the "hood of Helena." Sonya said the men in that area are constantly in and out of prison.

"Y'all may not realize it in Minnesota, but in Alabama there's still a lot of racial strife and they'd want to know why the white chick was up here," Sonya said. "And I even got pulled over by a policemen, a new policemen was on the force and he didn't know who I was, and he pulled me over because I was in the hood and he thought I was down here, like a soccer mom getting her fix."

If I didn't know Sonya, I may have made the same assumption.

We pulled up to a house where a man never let his pit bull off its chain in the front yard. The dog had become mentally unstable. As we pulled up to the house, Sonya warned us about the man's hostile attitude. She recommended we leave our cameras in the vehicle.

I stepped out of the SUV and the pit bull ran out from its house, pulling a length of chain behind him until it reached the boundary of his existence. The chain snapped tightly before bowing heavily back toward the ground. The dog's jowls curled up as he stared me down with ghost-like eyes.

The man walked down from the house, rubbing his protruding belly, and Sonya asked him if the dog would let us get close to him.

"Ummm," the man cocked his head and raised his brow. "Maybe."

This was one of the guys Sonya said was in and out of prison, so I watched his body language closely. All I noticed was the way he slowly stretched his jaw open and shut, some sort of tick. His fingernails were extra long and reminded me of a boy I went to high school with who kept his pinky nail extra long so he could snort drugs from it.

Sonya got out and grabbed a bag of dog food from the back of the SUV. Eli nosed at her hand before she closed the door. She handed the man the bag and asked if he needed any dog bowls, a question he deferred to his young son who was trying to tame the pit bull.

"How about some candy?" Sonya winked at the boy.

The boy smiled and Sonya said she would bring him some.

"Y'all take care," she said. And we left.

She could have given the man a lecture on how to treat his animals, but she was playing the long game, hoping to build a relationship before entering her opinion on how he went about his business. It was likely a combination of her faith and experience that kept her from getting hot under the collar. Certainly admirable.

We watched her interact with several people in the same manner. She was laying bricks, one by one. Building trust.

We pulled up to an abandoned property just down the road, and before we got out, I had Sonya read the sign posted on a tree near the property line.

"No trespassing, violators will be shot, survivors will be shot again," Sonya made her signature clicking noise and smiled at me. "I've been coming for years, so far no one's shot at me. A lot of puppies are born underneath this house, so I just have to be sure none are in distress. They know I'm here for the dogs, I'm not here for their drug junk."

We walked through the weeds toward the house, stepping around piles of garbage and bent metal.

"This may be a good spot for y'all to camp out tonight. There's a bathtub," Sonya teased, pointing to a rusted bathtub filled with garbage.

We told her we were thinking the same thing.

"Lulu! Lulu!" Sonya called out in her high, calming voice. "There's a stray named Lulu that we've been trying to catch for years."

We followed Sonya as she crawled down under the house to look for Lulu. There was a pile of hay under the house and several bowls she had put there for the colder winter months. If she knew a dog was living there, she would change out the water frequently. One of the bowls was filled with stagnant, green water, so I imagined if there was a dog there, it had either been rescued or moved on.

After a minute of searching, we surrendered and continued along Sonya's rescue route. She didn't like wasting time.

Not far down the road, Sonya spotted Lulu, plump full of babies waddling near a royal blue, doublewide trailer.

Lulu trailed off into the thick woods alongside the house where we couldn't get to her, so Sonya put out a bowl of water and food, hoping to lure her back. She got down on her knees and peered through the bushes at Lulu, who was wagging her tail.

"If you have something to wag about then I guess we all do," Sonya flirted. "Because we're not hungry, hot, and pregnant and live in the woods."

Sonya planned to pay a trapper to come back for Lulu, who was proving to be her most difficult rescue of the year. The dog had given birth to 70 puppies, and those were just the ones Sonya had counted. It made me realize how quickly the number of stray animals can multiply if owners neglect to spay and neuter their pets.

We pulled into a driveway where a woman was sitting in her yard on a foldout chair, talking on her cellphone. Sonya leaned out the window to ask if the woman had seen a brindle dog, which she had not.

"Do you need any dog food?" Sonya asked as she pushed the vehicle into park. The woman said dog food would be nice, so Sonya climbed out and opened the hatch to grab a big blue bag of Purina.

"Miss Sonya!" a young, overweight, black boy ran up to give Sonya a hug.

The boy, Leon, was used to Sonya coming around and often helped her catch stray dogs.

"How are you? I still have Lucy Goose at my house," she said, referring a dog Leon helped Sonya rescue.

The boy smiled, tugged at his waste band to pull up his plaid pajama pants, and then asked Sonya about the dog she had in the back of the SUV.

"This is Eli. He's a superhero," she said. "He helps to rescue other dogs."

The boy smiled.

A wiry, ankle-high dog ran up behind Leon as he carried the blue bag of dog food to his mother.

"Is she up to date on shots?" Sonya asked.

"She hasn't had 'em since she was three months," the woman replied, lowering her cellphone from her ear.

"And she's about to have puppies," Leon added.

"She's about to have babies?" Sonya paused, looking surprised. "Ok, I can't give her shots while she's pregnant, but I'll come back in four weeks to give you some de-wormer stuff for the babies."

Leon disappeared into the house with the bag of dog food, then came back outside a moment later with two of his older family members in tow, both male, and in their twenties. We explained to them the focus of our documentary, and the more talkative brother said he helped Sonya rescue a pit bull when Leon wasn't around. I asked him what he thought about dog fighting and animal abuse in general.

"Crazy, crazy, crazy," he said. He didn't try to deny its existence like most people we encountered. He knew it happened and genuinely thought it was disturbing. I couldn't help but think his viewpoint had something to do with Sonya and Two by Two Animal Rescue.

I swiveled my camera around quickly to record Sonya giving a small dog a syringe full of de-wormer. Eli escaped from the back of the SUV and ran over to wet noses with the little mamma dog.

"E!" Sonya said. "Load in the back, baby."

We all shuffled back in the SUV, but before we left, Leon came running toward the car with his much skinnier friend.

"Hey!" Sonya rested her head in her hand and smiled at the boys like a flirtatious cartoon batting her eyelashes. "I've got a deal for ya."

Both boys crowded the car window and studied our camera equipment.

"Yeah, how much?" the skinny boy asked.

Sonya threw her head back and laughed, then asked if the boys had seen the "tiger striped," brindle dog.

"Yeah, Spike," Leon said.

"Oh, y'all call him Spike?" Sonya sounded hopeful.

"We can get him today," the skinny one said. "How much is the deal?"

"How much do you need?" Sonya asked, but before she could let them answer, put up her finger and said "Be reasonable, be gentle."

"20 each," Leon said.

"20 each? You got it," Sonya agreed, and before they could discuss the deal further, the boys sprang from the car and started running down the road in search of the dog. The whole interaction lasted 42 seconds, which made me believe it wasn't a unique occurrence, but one of many deals made in the past.

Sonya sat back in her seat and let out a gleeful laugh before shifting the vehicle in reverse.

"We'll see. We'll see if they can cough up Spike this quick. It sure would save me a lot of days of looking for him." Sonya paused, rested her elbow on the side of the car. "20 bucks," she laughed.

"I feel bad, I forgot his name and he remembered mine," Sonya turned to me to say that a lot of the boys in that neighborhood have nicknames. Leon's, she said, is Fatso.

Poor kid, I thought.

The skinny boy pointed to where he saw the brindle dog earlier, then called back to Leon to "hurry up and run."

"If you catch him fast I'll throw some candy in the deal," Sonya yelled out the car window.

A big black dog came running out toward the SUV and barked heavily at Sonya as it ran past.

"Hey! Hey little Nutmegs," Sonya said. When she told us she knew all of the dogs in the area, she wasn't lying. Nutmegs, I imagined, was either the dog's real name or the nickname Sonya gave to the dog that was actually named Meg.

Sonya had her head out the window looking behind the vehicle, calling out for Spike.

I saw a striped dog out ahead of us and asked Sonya if it was Spike.

Sonya gasped, nodded in agreement and opened the door to scoop up the pooch.

"Loverboy! What you doing?" she said. Then in the same voice she used with Eli, she started talking to him in singsong.

"We're going to the vet and we're getting snipped and clipped," she sang. "No more babies. Snipped and clipped. Snipped and clipped."

Sonya rubbed the dog all over, plucking several ticks from its ears, which she threw onto the pavement and asked Joe to step on.

"Can y'all give me a ride back home? That dog right there is mean," Leon pointed to Nutmeg who was at his heels.

"Man, give me the bat," the Skinny boy said, gearing up to hit the dog with a toy baseball bat.

"Don't hit him with the bat, that's what makes him mean." Sonya waved her arms in a grand gesture like a traffic cop trying to yield a fast-moving motorist.

Both boys hopped in the back of the car and Sonya drove slowly back toward Leon's house.

"Even though he actually ran to me I'm still going to pay ya'll because I wouldn't have known which house to keep looking at," Sonya said.

"Delightful," the skinny boy approved.

We pulled up to Leon's house and the boys spilled out. Sonya didn't have cash, so she said she would write them a check and their mom could take them to the bank. Joe stopped her and said he had cash and handed her two twenties.

"Twenty for you, and twenty for you," Sonya dished out the dough to the boys through the car window, finishing the deal. The skinny boy took off, but Leon lingered at Sonya's window for a moment longer, scratching Spike on the nose.

"I love Spike," he said.

Sonya asked him what he was going to do with his 20 dollars, and he said he was going to buy candy. They discussed his favorite color of Skittles before parting ways. Sonya told us she would remember that he likes Skittles so she could bring him some another day as a good gesture. I could sense her repeating his name over and over, committing it to her memory.

"I can't imagine doing anything else that's this rewarding," Sonya shook her head and paused. "I just can't fathom it. If I had to I could practice law, but I just can't fathom having to put on the heels and sit in an office and argue and be a part of conflict resolution. That's just not something that makes my heart beat."

In my opinion, Sonya is practicing law, only from a different angle. Her form of down south justice isn't hot tempered, but relaxed and full of kindness, compassion and education. She is, without a doubt, a rare and infectious individual.

"What are we if we don't have hope?" Sonya settled in her seat and we retraced our route back to the parking lot we started from.

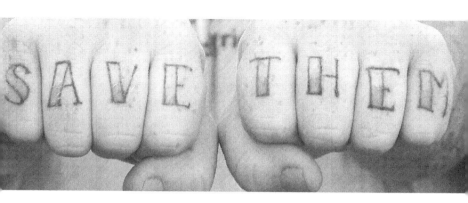

SAVE THEM

THE NUMBERS ARE STAGGERING. According the American Society for the Prevention of Cruelty to Animals (ASPCA), about 1.2 million dogs are euthanized every year in the United States. Nearly 10,000 of those come from Jefferson County, which includes Birmingham and its many suburbs. That number, however, is not all encompassing. As we learned, counties don't have to—and often don't—report their numbers.

At the time of our trip, Richard Burgess was the adoption rescue coordinator and euthanasia technician at the Birmingham Jefferson County Animal Control (BJC). He had the unsavory job of putting down thousands of animals as well as responding to cruelty situations. As the man behind the needle, Richard was used to taking heat from people who believed every animal should be saved, without exception. Even as an animal advocate, he said, sometimes the most humane thing to do is also the most difficult.

BJC's intake in 2012 was between 11,000 and 12,000, making it extremely difficult for Richard to play guardian angel for every single dog. And the reality is, a lot of dogs at BJC come from extreme cruelty situations and are very difficult to rehabilitate and rehome.

It's easy to assume that a euthanasia technician is heartless and numb, but I assure you, Richard is neither. He has a tattoo reading "SAVE THEM" stretched across his knuckles, each letter placed on one of his fingers so when he makes side by side fists, the message is clear. Menacing, yet peaceful.

On the day of our visit, BJC was busy handling 20 pit bulls that were seized from a property in Pleasant Grove. All of the dogs were malnourished and some had severe flesh wounds. The owner of the dogs was later charged on 19 counts of animal cruelty. The scene at BJC that day wasn't out of the ordinary; however, it was simply a reality, a day in the life.

Richard walked us through the facility, which was absolutely disorienting with noise and commotion. I filmed several dogs and the yellow signs attached to their kennels that read "Animal Cruelty" in red lettering along with a short list of what not to do with the dogs printed beneath. Joe tried monitoring audio through his earphones, but the electronic shrill of peaking audio levels caused him to lower the boom pole in surrender. It was too loud in the kennels and not worth going deaf over. I watched him shake his head as he quickly pulled his ear buds loose.

We followed Richard through a narrow hallway leading to a surgery room. A worker walked by trying to tame a mangy, hyper-energetic dog. We dipped into the room where a vet was pulling staples from a dog's healed flesh wound, the result of an embedded collar. I felt like I was at war in a triage tent, a general assessing the damage done to his troops.

"It's hard to fathom," Richard shook his head. "12,000 a year: strays and cruelties that come through our doors."

Richard is a big guy. He's tall, thick, tattooed and has gauged ear lobes. He's not someone to mess with. I asked him to talk straight to my camera like it was a dog fighter standing in his presence.

"Come fight me," Richard chuckled and nodded his head forward, signifying to me—and the audience of our film—that his invitation was real. "Punks fight dogs. If you have that mindset that you're going to let your dogs do your fighting for you and you're going to let your dog be that badass so that you can have this reputation, you're a punk, you're not doing anything. Real men do their own fighting," he said. "Come talk to me for 15 minutes, I'm either going to change your mind or I'm going to piss you off enough that something's going to happen and it's not going to be good on your end."

Richard grew up in the projects of Houston, Texas. He's been to prison. He's been stabbed. He's been that punk in a previous life.

"I've seen everything that's being done here, and back then it was considered to be okay," he said. "That's what fuels it. I've been there. I've seen it."

When he moved to Alabama, he got involved with Bama Bully Rescue, a group focused on rescuing and rehoming pit bulls. As the preferred fighting breed, the pit bull has gained a reputation as a dangerous animal and has even been banned in several cities across Alabama. Bama Bully Rescue works to inform the public that pit bulls have a bad reputation because of their irresponsible owners.

"Most people see a pit bull terrier and go 'Oh my God it's a pit bull,' because of what the media has made that dog to be," Richard said. "When people first see me, the heavy-tattooed guy, the big holes in the ears, and I'm a big guy, nobody would really look at me at first and say 'that guy cares about animals' or that guy does this or does that, and I can relate with that. I've been judged on my image for so long that me and the pit bulls kind of go hand in hand."

Richard is one of those rare people who have the ability to restore your hope in humanity. Because of where he's been. Because of what he's seen. Because he was able to turn his life around despite the odds. Standing next to him, I felt like less of a man.

I asked him what separates him from the punks who chose to continue their destructive lifestyle. His eyes glossed over and he told me about a Bama Bully Rescue event he helped organize where a young boy showed up to the booth and fell in love with their dogs. The boy didn't have a father.

"I wish back then I would have had somebody to step in," Richard explained how his father and stepfathers were all abusive and largely absent from his life. "I learned how to be a man by myself."

We had only been speaking with Richard for about 30 minutes and he already opened up to us about his less-than-ideal upbringing and the subsequent poor decisions he made as a young adult. I was envious of how open and honest he was. He had enough self-awareness to be comfortable telling us who he truly was and what ultimately guided him to a life of animal rescue.

I thought about the online trolls who tried to derail our documentary project on the basis that Alabama doesn't exhibit a culture of animal cruelty. How sad that must be to live in denial, to tell yourself over and over that your demons don't exist. Maybe if the truth came out, if more people were educated on the impact of animal cruelty, Alabama could lead the way in extinguishing a problem that is, in fact, nationwide. Maybe the whole state could take a page out of Richard's book and fess up, stand up tall and move on. You can only blanket the truth with so many lies before it rears its ugly head and bites you in the ass.

Richard was leaning against a counter as we filmed a BJC vet tending to a young mutt. He explained to us how animal control in Birmingham wish they could do more but their hands are tied.

"In the state of Alabama, dogs are basically listed as property. If there's a dog on chain starving to death and it doesn't have the proper shelter or the proper this or proper that, us as animal control officers have no authority to take that dog. We would have to involve police, and even with the police situation right now in the city of Birmingham, if you go out to an animal cruelty they legally have to leave a 24-hour notice on the door of who is violating this dog, and it gives them 24 hours to make any changes. Anybody can run out in a 24-hour time period and throw a fresh bowl of food and fresh bowl of water out and they've remedied the problem. Two weeks later the dog's back in the same situation it was in. But if I, as an animal advocate and animal rescuer, and also as an animal control officer, take the dog from this chain, I will be thrown in jail for theft of property," Richard gave us a look that said *ain't that some shit.*

What Richard described is not uncommon; It happened to a mural artist the summer we visited Alabama.

We met Joseph Giri (pronounced jeer-E) in front of a mural he just finished painting in Gadsden, Alabama. He was bald, wore circular, Lennon-like sunglasses, and had a white goatee. He looked like the artist version of Bruce Willis.

"I'm just a self-employed artist since 1986," he said. "Painter, sculptor, muralist."

"I was coming here to Gadsden for the last month painting this mural, which I call 'Fruit of the Gadsden Vibe,'" Joseph pointed to the mural behind him, which was alive with swirls of color surrounding men and women playing various musical instruments. It was beautiful and I could almost hear the music it depicted.

Joseph made the same 30-mile commute every day while painting the mural. Along his route, he stopped to look at a car at a closed-down car repair shop and junkyard.

"Out jumps this dog on about a 10-foot chain, almost no water, very little food, seriously underweight, underfed, mange, ticks, parasites," Joseph listed the indicators that led him—and any reasonable person—to believe the dog was not receiving proper care.

"So I started dropping off food for him every day, and petting him, rubbing him down, giving him some relief," he said.

Joseph then called animal control and was told to file a complaint with the city police. He did, but the situation never changed, and by that time, he had completed the mural and was continuing to assist the dog.

"I finally ended up taking him and tried to rehome him on Craigslist, and three days later they tracked me down and arrested me," he said.

Ain't that some shit.

Joseph posted his experience on his website:

"Late Weds. afternoon I was still getting my shop organized, cleaning out the truck, enjoying some time off, and the company of the Akita," Joseph wrote, referring to the junkyard dog. "I looked up from my tasks and noticed four official vehicles in my driveway ... two sheriffs cars, one police car, and an animal control truck ... boy it's a heavy feeling in the pit of your stomach when you see THAT in your driveway. My anxiety level and heart rate jumped into 5th gear ... "After they asked me my name, my first question was, 'Are you going to arrest me?' and they said yes. Whew! Never been there done that ... now my mind was whirling big time and I could see all the progress I've made in the last few years swirling down the toilet."

Joseph described the ever-familiar rollercoaster lifestyle of a struggling artist. In 1994, after finishing a major project in California, which led to more opportunities, he was in a head-on collision, which left him with compression fractures, no vehicle and a lawsuit. Seeing the police show up at his house that day resurfaced the same feelings of despair he had in '94.

"What I'm very thankful for is the fact that the officer from Piedmont who actually arrested me was a female who was also a Sergeant and very collected and calm. She was kind enough to handcuff me in front of my body and believe it or not she used Hot Pink handcuffs," Joseph wrote.

"My bond was $1,000 and I needed someone to co-sign on the bond, so I called my brother. Again I was fortunate that the bondsman recognized my name because one of the murals I painted in Anniston for the 50th anniversary of the Freedom Riders being attacked in Anniston, was behind the bondsman's office! He personally offered to drive up to get me out.

"We climbed into the Bondsman's car and he informed me he needed to pick up his other daughter who was nearby before going home and that he could give me a ride to my house. We went by an ATM and I paid him the $100.

"It was then that he told me that he knew me from the Bus mural project and that he also knew my father and brother. Oh the benefits of the small town life ... thank you Buddha. They dropped me off at home and he said that I had no further financial obligations on the bond. I gave him an extra $20 for the ride home.

"I stood in my driveway in a fugue state for awhile, just looking at the trees, grass, and my upcoming garden in the twilight. It was really hard to get my head around what just happened and all the intense experiences of the last few hours. That same sinking feeling that I'd thoroughly shot myself in the foot came back, but I reassured myself that I was older and ever so slightly wiser now and that I could get through this if I just controlled my tendency towards negative thinking and the resulting emotions. I also realized that I had been placed in a moral dilemma and I felt like I had to do something ... not because I was right and the law was wrong, or that I was a better person than the dog's owner. It was because taking no action was just wrong and the mental torture of not doing something was more pain than the consequences. That is what's driven me most of my life for better or worse."

I later followed up with Joseph about his case, and he told me it was dropped, but the dog got to stay with its owner and continue to be neglected.

What a mess. Animal Control has little legal grounds to prevent animal cruelty in certain situations, and if a concerned citizen steps in to correct the issue, they risk being thrown in jail and labeled a criminal.

All of this creates an environment that makes it extremely difficult to do the right thing, and that perpetuates a culture of animal cruelty. Richard knows it, Joseph knows it, and heck ... the sergeant who slapped pink handcuffs on Joseph probably knew it too.

AVRAL

HOUSE BILL 147 WAS PUT UP FOR A VOTE in the Alabama state legislature on the night of June 2, 2011. Representative Steve McMillan was an original sponsor on the bill.

"When the bill came up, I went to the microphone to explain it. Before I could even start explaining they all started yelling, 'Vote! Vote! Vote!'" McMillan said. "It just moved passage. It was gone."

The bill banned the use of gas chambers as a means of euthanasia in the state, earning animal rights activists a huge victory. Known as Beckham's Bill, the legislation is named after a dog that narrowly survived the gas chamber in the Cullman County Animal Control facility.

The group behind Beckham's Bill was AVRAL, a political action committee of which most everyone we met and interviewed was a member.

McMillan said the favorable response to Beckham's Bill was overwhelming. Typically, he said, new legislation doesn't pass on the first attempt; in fact, he's worked on bills that have taken more than 10 years to pass. He credits Beckham's Bill's success to AVRAL, which encouraged its members to call their representatives and speak in strong favor of animal welfare.

AVRAL's state chair, Rhonda Parker, is a professor at Samford University in Birmingham. She said the group started with just a handful of members in 2010, but over the course of a year, acquired more than 5,000 new members in all 67 counties. Today, they stand more than 10,000 members strong.

Before AVRAL, rescue efforts in the state were fragmented, and many rescuers and concerned citizens like Joseph felt alone in the fight. AVRAL unified their voices and provided them with yet another way to help advocate for companion animals.

"We have a lot of people in AVRAL who are homemakers, retirees, military people, firefighters, police officers. We have the educators, physicians, attorneys. So we have people who come from all walks of life, so they bring multiple perspectives to the group," Rhonda said.

AVRAL operates as part of a much larger system. There are statewide battles like passing Beckham's Bill, but also issues within smaller communities. One of the largest municipal issues AVRAL is involved with is breed-specific legislation (BSL), which is the blanket term for laws that regulate or ban specific breeds of animals. AVRAL members, Rhonda said, are able to show city council members and mayors that BSL is costly and difficult to enforce.

According to the ASCPA, the first round of BSL in the 1980s coincided with a rise in pit bull ownership among gang members. The outlaw status of the pit bull encouraged ownership by irresponsible people, and in turn, perpetuated the breed's poor reputation.

Take, for example, the owner of the red-nosed pit bull from Cottondale who refused to have his dog spayed because he wanted to breed it somewhere in Joplin. BSL ties the pit bull breed to illegal behavior and creates a culture of cruelty and ignorance, leaving people like the Cottondale man believing his animals are nothing more than an investment in illegal activity. This environment, of course, takes shape slowly without people noticing. And when it creeps into the culture of a place, it's hard for people to understand why it's wrong.

The Centers for Disease Control and Prevention called BSL "inappropriate and ineffective" in a 2001 task force report. In response to a petition to ban BSL on a federal level, the Obama administration said it does not support such legislation, adding that "dogs of any breed can become dangerous when they're intentionally or unintentionally raised to be aggressive."

I think we can all agree: BSL does more harm than good.

Rhonda said many animal rights groups have visited Alabama, but it's been very easy for legislators to write them off as extremists. AVRAL, she said, is able to bridge the gap between extremists and realists and explain the impact of animal overpopulation, abuse and neglect in relatable terms.

"I mean that in the sense of economics," Rhonda said. "The entire animal control system is very costly."

In 2015, Huntsville budgeted just under two million in animal services, Birmingham budgeted 1.5 million, and Mobile just under one million.

When Alabamians—and the rest of the country—learn that their money will be better spent following more animal responsibility, Rhonda said, that's when real change can happen.

The economic argument, however, can be a two-sided coin. Speaking with representative McMillan, we learned that legislators, not surprisingly, are often pulled in many directions. The Alabama Farmer's Federation, McMillan said, is largely opposed to new animal legislation and has a huge presence in the state legislature.

"I think a lot of it can be compared to the NRA," he said, referring to the National Rifle Association, which is opposed to any type of gun control. "Once you start it, where's it going to stop?"

"Working with the legislature, we found, is a very steep learning curve," Rhonda said. "We also found that legislators are very receptive, very open to hearing from their constituents. They were also, I think, rather surprised to hear from so many people in regards to animal rights issues."

It comes down to strength in numbers, which AVRAL has. Its members are beginning to enact change across the state in very different ways. As we traveled from county to county, we met a number of AVRAL members making small, yet meaningful, adjustments in their respective communities.

Lorna Aho is the president of the Macon County Humane Society, which she said should be called Macon County Rescue because they spend most of their time rescuing dogs from the local shelter, which in the rescue world is considered Band-Aid work; it's necessary, but only serves as a temporary fix.

Lorna enlisted the help of vet students from Tuskeegee and Auburn Universities, who she said are vital in making the humane society function successfully, even though some students have been told by professors that they can either be veterinarians or rescuers, but not both. In the summer, when students become less available, Lorna gets busier.

Not twenty minutes after meeting her, a white suburban pulled up Lorna's gravel driveway. A proper looking woman stepped out. The woman, Michelle, was a veterinarian and Lorna's neighbor. She opened the hatch of her suburban to reveal a chocolate-colored feral dog.

"She needs a little TLC and some medical care," Michelle said as she rubbed the dog's neck gently.

The plan was for Lorna to put the dog up in her empty kennel until the following week when Michelle would come back and bring the dog to her office to be spayed. Lorna was slightly annoyed that Michelle couldn't take the dog to her own property, but also very appreciative that she rescued it in the first place.

"Anybody who has a conscience ends up doing animal rescue in this area," Lorna told us after Michelle left.

After the vetting, the dog would need a foster, which would prove difficult to find since the vet students checked out for the summer. Either way, Lorna happily put the dog up in one of her quarantine kennels alongside her garage.

The timing of Michelle showing up when we were there was not a coincidence, but a reality that Lorna invited into her life when assuming the role as humane society president.

Lorna's home is situated on a beautiful plot of land surrounded by lush, rolling hills. Horses roam inside a vast fenced-in area, and when they stand still, the scene looks like a postcard and what outsiders likely imagine when they hear the Lynyrd Skynyrd song 'Sweet Home Alabama.'

Lorna, however, sounds nothing like a native Alabamian. Her thick British accent is a clear giveaway that she's a transplant from England. She uses phrases like *gob smacking* when describing the culture shock of moving to Alabama and words like *scuzzy* in reference to the old county pound. She's clean cut and slightly academic looking, but will surprise you with graphic imagery of what it's like to watch a dog die of Parvo or how, if it weren't for the support she finds in her community, she would surely slit her wrists from stress.

After playing with some of the rescue puppies in her yard, we crammed into Lorna's Volkswagen Beetle and she drove us to the location of the old county pound, which was a grungy outdoor run of six pens and the place Lorna said Michael Vick should have to spend his time when he's not playing football.

"He should be living in county pen seven," she said with a toothy, British grin.

There is a new shelter now, which Lorna said is nicer but has much of the same issues in its management.

The county workers at the pound, she said, have weekends and holidays off and will call Lorna before holiday weekends and ask her to rescue the dogs; otherwise they will be put down, even though their seven-day hold isn't up.

"We go on holiday and the dogs all get to die. Woohoo," Lorna said mockingly.

What she was explaining was nothing new to us, and to be honest, bored me slightly: Another county with the same gross neglect and indifference for companion animals was mundane and ubiquitous. I wanted something juicy, something shocking ... that story with blood and fire that leads the nightly newscast.

We pulled up to the old county pound and filmed the now-empty runs as Lorna described her dream for the future of Macon County Humane Society.

"We have had talks about building an adoption facility that could serve as a public interface," she said, referring to the county offering a 100-year lease on a piece of property where they could build a facility with the help of donations and grants. "That's certainly the way forward, that's where I'm headed."

"My time is far better spent organizing than it is slinging puppy poo," Lorna said. "As my therapist always says, 'Just because you can, doesn't mean you should.'"

I focused my camera on a dog treat nestled among wrappers, a nametag and a green pen in Lorna's cup holder and realized the headline of Lorna's story doesn't come from a singular, shocking incident of heroism but is crafted from the details and small steps she takes toward improving her community. It's the puppy-poo slinging, the addition of more kennels in the yard, the enlisting of new volunteers ... the dog biscuit in the cup holder, that mark of a prepared humanitarian doing more than any one-act rescuer.

Jane is also an AVRAL member. She attends AVRAL events and petitions her representatives on animal issues. She has rescue dogs of her own, fosters and a full-time job on the side. Jane, however, is not her real name. She wishes to remain anonymous for well-warranted reasons: Jane is a vigilante.

We followed her on a late-night mission—or crime, depending on your interpretation of well-intentioned, illegal acts—to rescue a dog that had been chained in the owner's backyard woods for four years straight, information Jane acquired from the owner's neighbors. To add a level of complexity, the owner of the chained dog was a homicide detective in Birmingham.

I flipped on the car light to accent Jane's hair and create dimension in my video frame, which worried her until I assured her that her face was still completely blacked out.

Jane lit a cigarette and rolled her window down.

"What are we doing?" I asked her.

"We are going to the Waffle House to get waffles," she joked, masking the fact that she was about to commit a crime.

"We're really hungry right now," she added with a chuckle.

After the corny analogies and code speech were done, I decided to play devil's advocate and ask the tough questions. I asked her if she considered talking to the man in person before resorting to theft.

"I don't think that would be wise," Jane said. "I know him and the kind of person he is and it would do no good to confront him, and the dog would be there his whole life."

"There are no laws to protect the dogs, so sometimes we have to take matters into our own hands," she said, tapping the end of her cigarette out the window.

I've seen vigilante scenarios played out on cop shows before. An armed robber enters a gas station, waving a pistol in the store clerk's face until a customer tackles the masked mugger. But those were random acts of opportunity, not premeditated acts of justice. I felt dirty and slightly responsible for whatever was about to go down.

We pulled into the driveway of a neighboring house, the property of which abutted the backyard of the homicide detective's yard. A small creek served as the property line, which Jane said would be tricky to navigate.

Armed with a handgun and a pack of hot dogs, Jane stepped out of the vehicle and disappeared into the darkness. Joe and I followed from a safe distance and decided to stop at the creek so we could maintain a separation between filming a crime and participating in one. We didn't know if that logic had any legal standing, but it helped to ease our nerves.

We hid behind a tree and filmed Jane's silhouette as she stopped to assess the situation. The dog, a squatty bulldog, was barking and could draw attention to us at any minute. We could see figures move about in front of a television inside the homicide detective's home.

Jane moved out of view and we heard her cross the creek behind enemy lines. We squinted in her direction but could see nothing. Every second we sat in silence seemed like eternity. Then Jane's flashlight beamed and scanned the area in front of her where the dog was barking. She threw the hotdogs at its feet, which silenced the barking.

I felt relieved. No barking dog, no more reason for suspicion. I looked back toward the house and just then, the television clicked off and the figures moving inside were no longer silhouetted by its oscillating glow.

Shit, I thought.

"That light just went off," Joe whispered, reaffirming what I already knew.

I immediately flashed back to the times when my family dog was barking at the window. I would turn the lights in the house off to eliminate glare so I could survey the yard for potential danger. Mostly, I knew there was nothing outside to be afraid of and was simply entertaining my dog, but there was always that possibility of a real threat, something other than a squirrel scratching alongside the house. I imagined that was exactly what the detective was doing, playing the fearless authority figure of the household surveying his territory for signs of intruders. I quickly moved my sweaty palm over my camera's LCD display to block the light from hitting my face. After waiting for movement from Jane for what felt like 10 minutes, but in reality, was more like 45 seconds, Joe and I shuffled back to the vehicle where we agreed that we were photographing the storm damage, which became our go-to excuse for trespassing.

Not long after, Jane ran toward us with the dog in tow, which didn't seem to be putting up a fuss. We jumped in the vehicle and sped off, Jane and I in the front and Joe in the back with the dog.

"You're alright," Joe comforted the big bulldog, whose white and tan coat had turned brown from years of lying in dirt.

"I thought he was going to bite me at first, he was scared, growling," Jane said. "The hot dogs did it."

"They have a big, nice house, a big yard, and they put the dog in the woods. And he's been there for years," Jane sighed, clearly frustrated but relieved at the same time. "He's free!"

Jane managed the steering wheel with her wrists as she teased a cigarette out of its pack. She had already arranged for a driver to transport the dog to Texas. She reminded me of a skydiver who relied on the adrenaline of a jump to feel alive. I wondered if her vigilante behavior, which began out of a need to save dogs, was transforming into a need to feed herself with that rush of adrenaline.

"Now what would y'all have done if they had come out and got me?" she asked, slightly annoyed that we retreated to the car when the lights in the detectives home went out.

"We were filming tornado damage," Joe said, continuing the banter of ignorant denial from earlier.

Yeah, I thought, *those damn Waffle Houses are hard to find.*

LOUIS VUITTON
THE PIT BULL

DO YOU EVER HEAR A MEDIOCRE SONG ON THE RADIO and wonder how it ever topped the charts? That's what came to mind when I met Louis Vuitton, the poster dog of animal abuse in Alabama.

I don't mean to dilute the shock value of his life story, but in reality—and probably to most people's amazement—it's really not that different from thousands of abuse cases across the state.

The difference: Louis' abuser was sentenced to 9 1/2 years in the Alabama Department of Corrections, the harshest punishment for animal cruelty in the state.

Louis Vuitton's new owners, William and Dee Hartley, created a Facebook page for Louis and wrote a short autobiography from the dog's perspective.

"Around 8:30 in the morning on September 7, 2007, in a fit of rage at his mother, Juan Daniels (who was 20 at the time) tied me to a fence and began beating me with a stick. The stick soon broke and he picked up a shovel and began hitting me with the blade all over. I had cuts to the top of my head and nose from the side of the blade.

"He then doused me with lighter fluid and lit me on fire! The fluid ran down my back and puddled on the ground beneath me where it became a pool of flames. I was tied so I had no way to escape the flames!

"My back left leg was totally engulfed and the pain was so intense I tried to bite my leg off. The pads of my feet and toenails were all burned off as well as my ears. My nose, eyes and forehead were badly burned, not to mention my entire underside where the flames were the most intense.

"Fortunately, the 13-year-old sister was in the backyard and witnessed the horrific scene. She ran into the house and called 911. The Police and Fire Departments responded to the call. A Humane Officer from the Montgomery Humane Shelter was contacted by the 911 operator as well and arrived soon after because he happened to be three minutes from the scene. When he got in the backyard, the flames were out and I remained chained to the fence with my little body smoking.

"The Humane Officer's name is Matthew Cooper and he gently removed the collar and led me to his waiting van where he would take me to a local Veterinarian to be euthanized, hoping all the while that I would not slip into shock before I could be delivered to Golden Animal Hospital for relief from the unimaginable pain.

"Matt sped across town as fast as possible and found that each time he would look over his shoulder at me, I would respond by wagging my tail. He called ahead and Dr. Holladay Simmons and the technicians were all waiting for me. When I was led in the backdoor by Matt, the first thing they all noticed was that, even in excruciating pain, my tail was wagging.

"I was placed in an exam room and Dr. Simmons did a quick exam and went to prepare the medication to euthanize me. She came back into the room and my tail, again, was wagging. She left, composed herself, then went back in but my tail was still wagging...

"Tears flowing, she left the room again, regained her composure and went back in to find her tech sitting in the floor with me in her lap. With full-thickness burns over 70% of my little body, I looked into her eyes with hope and determination.

"At that point, she made me a promise that she would fight to save me as long as I would fight to survive. We formed a tremendous bond! That was the day that my previous life and "Cain" died, and "LOUIS VUITTON" was born.

"My recovery was slow and, as with any burn patient, excruciatingly painful. Along with daily treatments and sloughing of dead skin, there were many skin grafts. I suffered deep muscle injuries to my back left leg from when I tried to bite it off. With no skin on the pads of my feet, *walking was very painful and because of the severe burns to my little belly and sides, it was too painful to lie down. The wounds were so raw many nights the staff at Golden Animal Hospital went home in tears because they feared I would not survive the night. But each morning I met them with my tail wag.*

"Gradually, I began to show improvement. I was also transported to a Vet in Auburn, AL, to have a canine tooth removed because the tooth was split straight up into my jawbone from one of the shovel blows.

"My story was not released to the media for the first two weeks because my survival was in question and the Shelter wanted to wait until I began showing some improvement. All the while, Juan Daniels was 'on the run' and law enforcement officials from all over the State of Alabama were searching for him."

On our way through Montgomery, we met with Louis and his owner, William Hartley, at a retired Montgomery police officer's home. The officer, Richard Koerner, had a rescue dog that was used for hunting but was discarded after the hunting season ended and left to fend for itself on the side of the road.

"Louis!" William was seated on Richard's sofa when he called to his dog, which was surveying the home for new scents.

Louis came running around the corner, tongue hanging from his mouth and tail wagging in high tempo, thumping against furniture. A small patch of fur, which somehow survived the flames, stood out on his back left leg like a small island on the map of an ocean. His skin was red and patchy and his ears were jagged, but Louis exuded nothing but confidence and playfulness.

William tried to show us the extent of Louis' injuries, but the dog flopped onto its back and begged for a belly rub. Louis didn't want to sit still, so I followed him back to a laundry room where he showed me his food and water bowls. He lapped up a happy mouthful of water before leading me back to the living room where William was ready to tell me about his now-famous rescue dog.

William explained how Juan Daniels was charged under the Pet Protection Act (Gucci's Law). Implemented in 2000, the act made first-degree cruelty to a domesticated dog or cat a felony punishable by up to 10 years in prison and a $5,000 fine.

"The reason that the penalty needed to be increased was because that's just where they start." William paused to stop Louis from whining. "It's statistically proven that they'll abuse children or other adults."

A study by the Massachusetts Society for the Prevention of Cruelty to Animals (MSPCA) tracked the criminal records of 153 individuals prosecuted by the MSPCA for 20 years—10 years before the abuse and 10 years after—and found that 70 percent of the people who committed violent crimes against animals also had criminal records for violent, property, drug or disorder crimes.

The study also used a control group of nextdoor neighbors and showed that people who abused animals were five times more likely to commit violent crimes against people.

When Juan Daniel's came up for parole in August of 2010, his family argued that he should be able to continue with his life, dismissing his crime as less severe because the victim was a dog. Here is Louis' account of that day, written by his owners.

"My parents were notified by the Alabama Department of Pardons and Parole that Juan Daniels came up for Parole and a hearing was set for August 24. My parents could not believe that this would even be an option for that monster. It was all over Facebook and the Internet as soon as it was posted by the Parole Board.

"An incredible lady in Chicago named Stacey Paige had started an online petition to stop Daniels' parole. The first time my mom went to the petition site it already had over 5,000 signatures from all over the world! She could not believe so many people were aware of my case. She was contacted by Stacey who was hoping to drive to Montgomery for the parole hearing. Unfortunately, she was unable to come, but there were others who drove down from Boston, Rhode Island, North Carolina, Birmingham and more.

"The Parole Board was flooded with so many letters against the Daniels' parole they had to assign a full-time clerk just to handle all the correspondence! As is the case with a parole hearing, the victim is allowed to appear before the Board to express opposition, in this

case our local District Attorney and Attorney General's Office had it cleared for me to appear before the Board—the first time in U.S. history that a dog appeared as the victim!! My parents said I was PERFECT! I knew it was something serious and was on my very best behavior.

"All the news crews were there, including Associated Press. The story of a dog appearing before a Parole Board went worldwide—literally! It was reported on news broadcasts all over the world! My parents were so incredibly proud of me."

More than 60 law enforcement officers and animal rights advocates stepped up to bat for Louis at Juan's parole hearing. Holladay Simmons, the veterinarian who saved Loui's life, silenced the room with a gripping testimony.

"I don't claim to be a great orator, so I ask for your patience. My name is Dr. Holladay Simmons and I am the veterinarian who has treated Louis throughout his ongoing recovery. I have been working with animal rescue groups and the humane society for over 10 years and have witnessed horrid examples of man's inhumanity on almost a daily basis. However, I had never witnessed anything even marginally close to the cruelty that I saw on that September day that Louis came to me. It affected me to the core and I lost a little part of faith in humanity that day.

"He was literally still hot to the touch when he arrived. His eyes were actively swelling shut in front of us, where his face and eyelids had been so badly burned. His toenails and pads were melted and burned away from standing in the lighter fluid. Large chunks of flesh were missing from his sides where he had torn it away with his own teeth in a futile attempt to escape the horrific pain. The inside of his nose and throat were burned from inhaling the heat and flaming fumes, and yet, the first thing he did was squint up at me and wag his tail, a completely innocent soul asking for comfort. And really, as much as I want justice for my precious Louis, I believe that this case is just as much about the protection of the innocent.

"Statistics show us that a large percentage of violent offenders start by abusing animals. Juan Daniels lacks any ability to feel empathy toward another living thing, and because of this, he will continue to torture and abuse. So I implore you all, please protect us. Protect yourselves. Protect our society and most of all, protect our innocent ... our children and our animals. They have no voice but ours. We have an ethical, a moral, and a legal obligation to protect those who cannot protect themselves. So, I beg you, please, today, vote to deny this man parole and help us in our continuing fight to protect the innocent among us."

Juan's cousin, according to an Associated Press report from that day, pled for Juan's release because he was behind bars with "folks who committed more extensive crimes than he committed"

Juan's mother, Vellica, begged the board for leniency but was met with an abrupt response from Bobby Longshore, the presiding Parole Officer at the hearing.

"M'am, he's not getting out even if he was in prison for only stealing a lawnmower," Longshore said.

In the end, Juan was his own worst enemy. He had nine disciplinary actions taken against him in prison before his parole hearing. His behavior in prison, coupled with the severity of his crime, ultimately led the board to vote unanimously to deny an early release date.

He was, however, released on good time in November 2013. Less than two years later, he made headlines again; this time, for the death of a child.

Aiden Howard, a 6-year-old boy, was watching cartoons at the Plaza at Centennial Hill Apartment in Birmingham when Juan Daniel ran his SUV through the wall. Aiden died 10 days later in the hospital.

"[Aiden] just didn't have time enough to get out of the way, and it ran over him and caused significant brain damage," Aiden's aunt, Phadra Stewart, told news reporters from WSFA.

Montgomery County District Attorney Daryl Bailey, when interviewed by WSFA, blamed the criminal justice system for letting an offender like Daniels out on good time.

"How in the world they keep letting these individuals out under the guise of good time is unbelievable, and it shouldn't happen," Bailey said. "When you have a violent offender who has amassed that many disciplinaries while he was incarcerated, they shouldn't get good time. They shouldn't be released back out into the public to do harm to another citizen."

Animal cruelty affects more than the animal, more than the rescuer, more than the taxpayers wallet, and more than a study correlating animal abuse with other domestic crimes. It leaves a permanent stain on society and immeasurable pain on innocent families.

Aiden was in the first grade. He loved football. But he never was given a fair shot at a future. He became another tragedy of the culture of animal cruelty.

William and Dee Hartley are often asked what Louis would do if he saw his abuser again.

"He would lick his face," they say, which makes my heart flutter and fists unclench just long enough to realize that companion animals have a tendency to love but are often not given that opportunity.

TOO MUCH

JOE AND I MET WITH BRANDT GARRISON, AN ANIMAL RESCUER who was our age, at a bar in Tuscaloosa. We were surprised to learn that she adopted a blue nose pit bull from Bonnie, the same one we helped Bonnie rescue during our first trip in Alabama. We teased her for changing the dog's name from Blue Bell—Bonnie's choice of ice cream—to Tut, which to us, sounded flat and dull.

A group of college-aged guys walked in and sat down at the bar next to us. They wore bright-colored shirts that begged for attention. After listening to our conversation, one of the guys joked about beating his dog. Sometimes, he said, a dog just needs a good beating.

Joe explained to them the focus of our documentary, and Brandt argued with them about humane treatment. The most talkative of the trio took several drinks and continued to make light of animal cruelty, forming what he thought to be philosophical arguments, which he accented with snide laughter and eye rolls.

I wanted to walk over to him, grab a fistful of his hair and slam his head against the bar. I knew if I joined the conversation, my short temper might cause me to do just that. So I kept my mouth shut.

Rotating my beer on its coaster and half listening as Brandt bickered with the man-children, I lost myself to another daydream. It's something I've been told I do often: Joe recalls several instances working with me at our college newspaper where he and others tried yelling my name in unison to get my attention but with no success. Sometimes—oftentimes—I zone out completely. I've never been able to determine whether that particular characteristic is a defect or useful defense mechanism.

I wondered if that same feeling, that sense of being overwhelmed, was what caused so many people to ignore the plight of animals in the South. It's easy to coast through life with blinders on, and maybe that blissful ignorance was the problem. Maybe Alabamians were conditioned over time to look the other way, to see a dog as an inanimate object. I didn't know if it was right of me to blame them, so I chose to ignore.

I went to bed that night with a headache.

Driving South to Mobile, I became frightened. We were passing dead animals alongside the interstate, just as we had months ago, but this time I didn't feel a thing. I don't know if I was numb, indifferent, or cloaking myself in blissful ignorance, but I was afraid I was slowly becoming a part of an avoidance culture, and that thought weighed heavily in my stomach.

In Mobile, we were reacquainted with Robbie Fitzgerald, President of the Safe Haven Animal Care Kennels (SHACK). She was in the process of converting two old buildings on 5 acres into an animal rescue facility. The Shack, at that time, was a small 800-square-foot building sandwiched between a Hardees and a Super 8 on a busy street.

Joe and I parked the SUV and met Robbie with our cameras mounted and rolling. We had learned, from our previous visit, to film what we could when we could because Robbie moves through her day quickly.

When we showed up, she was running from kennel to kennel, taking care of her morning routine before beginning her full-time job. A Shack volunteer flipped several dog crates over on a slab of concrete and began spraying them down with a pressure hose. I watched as she swept across their plastic bottoms, sending flecks of poop flying in all directions. I had to tiptoe around a stream of dirtied water as it rolled across the concrete toward my feet.

Robbie and Joe compared the amount of dirt on their clothes, and I took a picture of them together to document the messy nature of animal rescue compared to the messy nature of living on the road.

Robbie bent down to pet a female pit bull that had been tied to a computer cord before it was rescued. She cried but took a deep breath to compose herself. I noticed she had slightly more gray hair near her temples from when we met her six months prior. Rescue was wearing Robbie down, and I wondered if she had time enough to stop to realize it.

A woman walked over from the Hardees parking lot to one of the Shack kennels where she seemed very interested in a particular dog. I asked her if she was looking to adopt and she told me the dog in the kennel looked exactly like her old dog.

She introduced herself as Marquitta Holyfield, an older black woman who was wearing a flower-printed dress. She smiled at me with her big brown eyes, which began to gloss over. Curious, I asked her what happened to her dog.

"Well, my neighbor rung my doorbell and told me that my dogs were dead," Marquitta paused and made eye contact with me. "I went to look out the door and my dogs were hung on a tree."

Someone, for reasons Marquitta still can't comprehend, decided to hang her dogs by their necks from a tree in her front yard. I tried to think of possible reasons for such violence but came up blank: Marquitta didn't look like someone who was in debt with the wrong people. She was a well-kept, polite woman with a love for animals.

Tears began to pool in her eyes and she covered her mouth with her hand, flashing back to when she found her dogs hanging in her front yard. With as much sympathy as possible, I asked her why someone would do such a thing.

"I have no idea," she said. "I really loved that dog."

Marquitta said that after the incident, the lord blessed her with two new dogs: Ike and Tina.

"They ended up killing Ike," she said.

They? Who were these people? Was hanging a dog part of a gang initiation?

Marquitta was clueless, but she also didn't seem surprised. When Ike was hung, she had to watch him cough up blood until he eventually passed away, a memory she relayed to us far too passively. Like she had become accustomed to people killing her dogs.

Her sorrow quickly turned to anger as she explained to us how many times she's seen animal abuse in the two separate neighborhoods she's resided within Mobile. People fight their dogs and will do anything to them, she said.

"Do you hear of it or do you see it?" I asked her how she found out about people fighting their dogs. She smiled at me nervously, trying to decide how much information she was willing to share. She looked off toward the Hardees before turning back to me and admitting to seeing dog fighting first hand.

"Why do they do it?" I asked.

She gave me the same nervous smile.

"For the money. They do it for the money," she said, and then told us she better get going before she starts crying again.

I watched Marquitta walk back toward the Hardees, carefully lifting her dress to step down from a cement curb. I felt terrible for her and for people in her same position. She knew what was going on and who was responsible for it but was scared to say anything further, fearful that *they*—whoever *they* were—might graduate from harming more than just animals.

Seeing the pain in Marquitta's eyes made me realize that not everyone is numb and indifferent to animal abuse. They see it, they know who's doing it, but standing in the way of it could mean risking their lives. Instead, they smile nervously and choke back their tears. What more can they do?

I wish I could give all the Marquitta's of Mobile a hug.

"Yay, so exciting!" Robbie said as we pulled up to the new Shack location. A group of men were busy erecting a fence for animal runs. The group, recruited by Robbie's husband who owned a construction business, volunteered their time and resources.

"The small things that make us happy," Robbie said as she got out of the SUV to check the progress of the fencing.

She led us into one of the two metal buildings and spun around in the middle, elated by the amount of space. She was imagining the number of dogs she would soon be able to pull from death row in Mobile and house in that building, reveling in the sound of their playful cries.

The second building was even larger, and when Robbie opened the giant metal door, Joe said it looked big enough to build a NASA spaceship in. The building had a dirt floor that Robbie planned to cover with concrete after a grand opening garage sale, which would help pay for the job.

The new facility would have the capacity to hold up to 100 dogs, more than twice as many as their current location and a number Robbie was hesitant to share on camera because she didn't want to scare her volunteers away.

"It's hard for me to say no. We don't ever want to get over 75, but we will be able to facilitate up to 100," Robbie said. "Our goal is one day to have an empty piece of property that we have nothing to do with because there are no more dogs to be rescued."

One year later, the space was empty, but not because there were no more dogs to rescue.

In June 2013, one of the Shack's air conditioning units failed, causing two rescue dogs to die from heat stroke. The Mobile County Animal Control investigated the incident and in August obtained a search warrant. They found many sick animals on Robbie's property, some with bite marks. Robbie maintained that the animals were receiving monthly treatments and proper care.

"The breaker kicked and everyone yelled neglect," Robbie wrote to me in an online chat. "Rescue world is drama, David. We honestly got overwhelmed."

Animal control confiscated 53 dogs and 10 cats that day, leaving the Shack empty and devoid of its regular animal noises. No eager barking as volunteers greeted the rescue dogs, no pressure hose sweeping across the concrete floor, no trampling of dog feet in outside runs, no rustling of chains. The Shack, as Robbie new it, was shut down.

The incident represents how easy it is for rescuers to tackle more than they can handle. Robbie was working herself to death trying to save as many animals as possible, and if it weren't for her efforts, most of those 53 dogs would have been euthanized at the shelter.

Before the existence of the Shack's facility, I followed Robbie as she walked through the animal shelter in Mobile. I saw her break down in tears next to animals that had days to live. She wanted desperately to save those dogs but had nowhere for them to go. Those are the moments that motivated Robbie to build the Shack. She's not neglectful, nor is she the source of the problem. She dedicated 100 percent of her spare time and money working to reduce the number of euthanized animals in Mobile County. In my opinion, Robbie is a hero.

Was it unfair to the dogs that they weren't given the best care at the Shack? Sure. But the best care didn't exist. Robbie was their only lifeline and gave those animals a fighting chance. As she pointed out, however, it became overwhelming and was simply too much for one person.

No charges were brought against her, but Robbie's good name was dragged through the mud. A Mobile television news station broadcast the story, making her look like a criminal.

Losing her reputation, Robbie said, was worth the lives of the animals she saved.

Five hours north of Mobile we met another animal rescuer who, like Robbie, had also reached her limit.

Carrol Crocker didn't ask for a legal battle. She didn't ask to be homeless. She didn't ask to live in her garage with her dogs, and she certainly didn't ask for veiled threats against her life. But on a November morning in 2007, she got all of those things when her home, which served as her town's animal sanctuary, was burned to the ground by the hands of an arsonist.

Carrol agreed to meet with us in a parking lot visible to the public. I could tell from the way she spoke that she was sizing me up, trying to determine if I was who I said I was. Trust didn't come easy to Carrol, and I was about to learn why.

We pulled off the highway in Rainsville, Alabama, onto a dirt parking lot where we were scheduled to meet Carrol.

"Rainsville, Alabama," she would later tell us. "The gateway to hell."

Carrol was a small, older woman with tightly cropped, white hair. She wore silver earrings that looked like plain wedding bands, a hooded sweatshirt and blue jeans. After looking us over, she told us to follow her.

It was raining when we pulled up to Carrol's property, so we ran under the cover of a tree to protect our camera gear.

"This was once my home," Carrol said as she lifted her arms to encompass the area where her home once stood.

The skeleton of a brick fireplace and the first layer of bricks outlining the perimeter of the once 3,000-square-foot home were all that remained. A group of goats were feeding from a pile of trash, lifting their heads occasionally to make noises at us.

Rainsville is located in DeKalb County in northeastern Alabama. Until 2008, the county had no animal shelter or animal control. Carrol, a retired flight attendant, filled that role. She was living in the home passed down through her family and was taking in stray animals. She skirted the home with new decks and porches for the animals to live and never turned down an animal in need. At times, her 5-acre plot of land was home to more than 100 dogs and cats, which Carrol paid thousands of dollars every year to vet and feed.

As word got out, people in the community began dumping their unwanted dogs on her property as if they were taking their trash to the local dump. Rainsville city officials even admitted to abandoning dogs at Carrols property. Taking her friend's advice, Carrol decided to incorporate as a rescue organization so she could receive charitable donations and defer the cost of rescue to thankful community members.

Her rescue organization, Green Acres Animal Sanctuary, became known as the county's animal shelter.

Then, new neighbors moved in and fought with her over property lines and complained about her animals. At that time, Rainsville had no leash law and no ordinance limiting the number of animals a person could have. So, by law, she was doing nothing wrong.

But then, Carrol said, things got really weird.

The city sent her a cease and desist order, stating that she was in violation of zoning laws ever since she incorporated as a rescue organization. Carrol later received a court order stating she could have no more than three dogs on her property at a single time.

She fought back, hiring an attorney and filing appeals, but to no avail. Her sister reached out to rescue groups in the region to help Carrol re-home the animals on her property.

And then, the fire.

"I couldn't get to 'em. I couldn't get to 'em." Carrol stood in the middle of what used to be her home, remembering the morning someone made an attempt on her life.

According to Carrol, the fire department, which is less than 5 miles from her home, took 30 minutes to respond, and when a fire truck did arrive, there was only one firefighter with it. By that time Carrol's home was fully engulfed in flames and the damage, along with the lives of more than 50 innocent animals, was irrevocable.

Weeks later, Carrol learned that the incident was under investigation, which she thought strange since nobody had contacted her. She went to the fire department and asked the chief why he had not been out to her property, and he told her that there was nothing to investigate because her home burned to the ground. She told him she was going to call the state, which made him nervous and willing to cooperate, but Carrol didn't trust him, nor did she trust any city official, so she forbid him from stepping foot on her property. A state fire marshal later investigated the scene and ruled the fire as arson.

At the time, city officials were rumored to be involved in selling stray dogs to a rescue group in Atlanta, and for good money: More strays on the street meant more money in their pockets. For that reason, Carrol said it was beneficial for them to shut her operation down. This of course is rumor, and has to be taken with precaution. However, the sequence of events tells a damning story: Rainsville was trying to push Carrol out of town. That part was clear.

"If you consider the place you live to be the gateway to hell, then why do you live here?" I asked Carrol the question that had been eating at me during our interview.

"Because I've got a job to do," she said.

Standing near the ruins of her home, Carrol looked like a soldier holding her position despite enemy fire: holding the line so the rest of us could rest easy. She didn't ask to fight that battle alone, but she did it anyway, and she did it with pride.

When I get stressed or overwhelmed, I feel a brief flutter in my heart that sends me into a short panic attack. My arms and legs tingle and become hypersensitive. It's my body's way of telling me *'Dude, slow the fuck down and breathe.'*

After living on the road, hearing countless stories of animal abuse and risking my own life trying to save a bait dog from another brutal attack, it was time to listen to that voice of reason and recalibrate my inner compass. My conscience would finally allow me room to breathe.

Joe and I drove East out of Mobile, taking the causeway over Mobile Bay. The sun reflected harshly off the water, as if hitting a million broken mirrors all rolling and changing angles. We then traveled south to Gulf Shores, where we decided to clock out for a few days and spend time digesting and reflecting on what we encountered along our journey.

In journalism school, we were taught to distance ourselves from the subjects of the story and to remain impartial in our reporting: It's fine to have an opinion, so long as that opinion doesn't appear in your work in the form of bias. We also learned of writers who were driven by a specific cause and completely partial in their work. People like William Lloyd Garrison who published The Liberator, an antislavery newspaper. Garrison used journalism as a tool of social change.

I was lying on the beach in Gulf Shores trying to decide what form of journalism I was practicing, where I landed on the spectrum between journalism and activism. Was I wrong to have an opinion and to let that opinion show in my reporting, and is that any less professional than rewriting press releases for an anchor to read in nightly news broadcast? The trip was becoming my own form of graduate school, where I was faced with deciding what kind of writer I wanted to become, or better yet, an opportunity to discover the writer I already was.

My hands were sticky from sunscreen and covered in sand, so I wiped them on my shorts several times before pulling my typewriter out of my backpack. Its antiquated mechanics fueled me with inspiration and made me feel more connected to the words on the page. I fed a piece of yellowed paper in the guides and began punching out a poem, one that allowed all the cynicism and confusion I was feeling to escape:

The Cynic Picnic
By David Cowardin

Too much to look at
Too much sand and too much water
Too much light to see

I've gone dry
Inspiration fell victim to the tide,
Swept under and sent tumbling to a coastal cavern.
I throw my body at the waves
But am not delivered to where I belong.
An emerald enigma gargles and
Spits me back to shore,
Dried and salted for the gulls and
Shaded eyes to pick apart.

Too much time
Too much ahead and too much behind
Too much to set and rise

I've lost track
Creativity took the hand of idle doom,
Drawn in to the path of monotony.
I go there and back, there and back ... gone.
A treasonous torch counts my strides and
Guides me to my knees
For the clouds and darkness
To swallow me whole.

Too much of nothing
Too much sitting and too much waiting
Too much of mindless matters

I've faded off
Curiosity died a conversation ago,
Cloned and cut with the cheapest smile.
I keep looking for an honest eye
But am spun and tossed in a frightful daze.
A deafening drivel leaves me
Stranded in company,
Forgotten and flattened
By a social stampede.

Too much ...
Too much dullness and too much haze
Too much in the way and in-between
Too much trial, too much of a mess to clean
Too much to ignore
... Too much to look away.

PART FOUR
BACK TO BONNIE'S

THE LIST OF NAMES IN MY REPORTERS NOTEBOOK WAS DRYING UP.
Three days of filming remained before it was time to drive back to
Minnesota where I was scheduled to work at the news station the
following week. Not knowing where else to go, we found ourselves
back in Greene County with Bonnie.

Bonnie's yard dogs ran alongside the RV as we pulled into her
driveway. We honked to signal our arrival, something Bonnie told
us to do so she could come outside before her dogs mistook us as
intruders. She gave us both a hug, which felt like a right of passage.
We had earned her approval, and more importantly, her trust. She
was happy to do more filming with us, but room in her kennels
was limited, which would in turn limit the amount of rescuing
we could do.

Joe and I spent that evening fixing a kennel on the corner of her
property that had caved in on itself. After rebending metal posts
and reinforcing its corners, the kennel was ready for new occupants.
We told Bonnie that we wanted to take some of her dogs back to
Minnesota to be put up for adoption, which she was happy to hear.
Any help is welcome, she said.

The next morning, we situated dog crates in Bonnie's SUV and
prepared our camera equipment as Bonnie stopped at the end of
her driveway to check her voicemail.

"I knew this was too good to be true," she said, lowering the phone and shaking her head. "Let me call this lady right quick."

The woman who called was reporting a dog that was emaciated and dying in her neighbor's backyard. The dog didn't belong to her neighbor but took refuge under the shade of a tree on his property. Bonnie told the woman she would take a look but couldn't guarantee she could be of help because her kennels were full.

"They're using me for a shelter," Bonnie said, referring to the Greene County commissioners, but was quickly interrupted by the woman who warned—threatened—Bonnie that if she didn't come and get the dog, her boyfriend was going to shoot it and dump it off in the woods.

"It's like ... are the dogs going to eat? Are we going to eat? Where does it stop here?" Bonnie said, trying to explain to the woman that the county does not employ her and that her work is voluntarily. "You got a million animals out here that need to be helped out and the kennel we've got is about full."

Every day is a psychological domino effect: If Bonnie agrees to help the first dog, then she's also committed to helping the others she finds along her drive, which is especially problematic when she has no space left in her kennels. But she always follows her morals over her own safety and judgment. God has a plan for her, she said, and will provide in this life or the next.

Knowing what she was getting into, Bonnie pulled out of the driveway to follow up on the first call of the day.

"She's saying this dog won't even eat or drink. So do I bring it back to my place and mix it in with my stuff? You see what I'm saying?" Bonnie cocked her head sideways and looked down the road with a tinge of regret in her eyes. She had been down this road before and knew the dog she was about to check on was beyond saving. I could tell she wanted to save herself another heartache by ignoring the situation, but she kept driving onward, working the steering wheel with one hand at 12 o'clock and letting her shoulders slouch forward. Her body sighed from the stress of working beyond her means.

We pulled up to the property where the dog had taken refuge and the homeowner unsaddled his riding lawn mower to greet us. His John Deere petered out in a cough as he walked toward us.

"Come here, I'll show you," he said, and then stopped to explain that the dog was likely used for hunting then subsequently abandoned. "You know what they do when deer season is over? I used to deer hunt that way and I've seen 'em do it, they just turn 'em loose."

"Yeah I know, they get through hunting a dog, and they turn it loose," Bonnie echoed the man whose thick southern accent protruded more than his pot belly.

We continued walking toward the backyard, passing a garden full of ripe tomatoes, which the man tried selling to Bonnie.

"Yeah, I'll get some from you, but I gotta see about this dog right now," Bonnie reminded him of the reason we were there.

I took short, fast steps and tucked my elbows in, trying to hold my camera steady as we followed Bonnie, who was moving quickly toward the dog.

"You guys, get a good shot of this," Bonnie pointed at the dog lying in the shade, eyes barely open, mangy, and emaciated. "This is some crap isn't it?"

I zoomed in on the sickly dog as Bonnie reached down to examine it, pulling its jowls up to looks at its teeth.

"This dog might be on his last leg. I mean, look at his teeth. His gums are white," she said, and then released his jowls, which stuck to his dry gums and refused to slide back into place. The dog's eyes winced in pain, but his tail wagged in a circle as Bonnie patted him on the head. She tried to turn the dog on its side, but its body was so stiff that his backbone was unable to hinge properly. It was drying up and slowly curling toward death. Bonnie lifted its ears, revealing a colony of ticks.

"That means he was a good hunting dog there. See them ears?" the man said excitedly, more interested in the dog's breed than its physical condition.

"Well, he might have been a good hunting dog but he damn sure wasn't taken care of," Bonnie spoke so fast that her voice broke at the end of her sentence like a boy going through puberty. She was hot under the collar and speaking from the throat with emotion.

"To me, that person needs to be taken to the woods, and let them hunt, and then their ass should have to starve to death," Bonnie threw her arm up and leaned in toward the man to be sure he was listening. From a distance, the interaction resembled a domestic dispute between neighbors fighting over property lines.

"Excuse me, but that's the way I feel now. You know I see this crap every day, I see this all the time and I don't have any patience for this," Bonnie turned her attention back on the dog and ran her hand along its collar until thumbing its tags, where the owners name was etched.

"Kenneth Johnson," she said with spite.

There was also a phone number on the tag, which the man said belonged to some sort of corporation. Bonnie wrote the number down and we walked back to the SUV. As we passed the garden of tomatoes, Bonnie told man she would be back to buy some from him soon.

Bonnie dialed the number and was greeted by an automated message system that told her the person she was trying to reach didn't have voicemail.

She told us the dog would need to be put down unless it found the strength to walk off and die in the woods on its own, a fact she accepted long before we arrived on the scene.

Kenneth Johnson, I thought, thinking of the owner named on the dog's tag. I wanted badly to find him so we could embarrass him on camera and then beat him with our tripods.

Bonnie looked composed as she put the SUV in gear, almost like she had already forgotten about the dying animal. The truth was her heartache grew heavier with every cruelty case. She knew she couldn't save the dog so she decided to investigate elsewhere, which proved to be her coping mechanism and way of distancing herself from her emotions. But all that heartache and distance between her inner and outer self was building up and manifesting itself through her body language. She moved her hand to 12 o'clock on the steering wheel and let her shoulders slouch forward again, watching the yellow divider lines pass beneath the SUV, fighting back the despair trying to claw its way out.

We drove slowly through a neighborhood Bonnie knew to be plagued with animal cruelty. She rolled her window down to listen for animals, whistling periodically to elicit a response from dogs hidden deeper in the woods.

She pointed to a group of young boys circled around a chained pit bull, one of which was hitting the dog with a tree branch.

"God damn you! Excuse me lord." Bonnie quickly rescinded her curse to the heavens.

"Can I get out with you?" I asked, already unbuckling my seatbelt.

"I don't give a shit," she said, giving us a glimpse into the darkness that was beginning to callous her heart.

I thought she was going to grab the branch from the boy and give him a whooping, but when she approached, she quickly put her emotions back in check. I didn't know if her ability to transition between fury and friendliness so quickly was the mark of a good investigator or a sign of a mental breakdown to come.

"Hey guys, is that your puppy dog?" Bonnie stopped short of the boys and put one hand on her hip to signify her authority and disproval of what was happening.

"Huh?" The boy with the branch cowered his way toward Bonnie.

"He's a pretty dog," Bonnie added before asking the boy to fetch his father from inside the trailer home. She made small talk with the other boys while their friend called for his dad.

"Good afternoon, sir," Bonnie greeted the dog owner, who had to hold his shorts up to keep them from falling down as he walked toward us. He was uncomfortable with our cameras but allowed us to film anyway, saying he had nothing to hide.

"What's your name, sir?" Bonnie asked.

"Roderick," he said, sitting down on the edge of a picnic table.

"I know you. I think we met before didn't we, Roderick? Had a meeting one time," Bonnie grinned, reminding Roderick of the time she caught him breeding two underfed dogs whose puppies he planned to sell to dog fighters.

Roderick was a backyard breeder looking to score easy cash. His prized dog, a beefy pit bull, was chained to a tree on the corner of the property. Its tongue hung from its mouth as it pulled against its heavy chain, which bowed and thudded against the ground. It looked healthy except for its left eye, which was squeezed shut. Bonnie peeled it open to expose an infection and told Roderick to take the dog to the vet immediately.

"I'll leave you a notice," she said nicely.

The group of boys then guided Bonnie into the woods behind the neighborhood to show her the other dogs in the area, all of which looked well.

She joked with them for a while, and when she had their full attention she asked the group of boys if they were nice to their dogs. They all nodded in agreement but looked at the bigger boy in the group nervously, a giveaway that someone wasn't telling the truth.

"Think about it," Bonnie said, addressing the bigger boy in the group. "What if somebody's pulling your ear? What if somebody's pinching the crap out of ya? Would that feel good?"

One of the boys pinched the bigger boy and they all laughed. The bigger boy swayed back and smiled nervously.

"That dog don't like it either," Bonnie said.

"I told you," one of the boys turned to the bigger one and reveled in the glory of being correct.

"Wait a minute," Bonnie put her hand up like a teacher trying to quiet her classroom full of students. "God wants us to be kind to animals. Do y'all believe in God?"

"Yes," the bigger boy said, looking down at his feet.

"Thank you. I do too. He wants you to be kind to animals. You know what he'd do? He'd get you if you don't be kind to animals," Bonnie warned, leading the boys back toward the trailer home where their sisters were splashing around in a small, above-ground swimming pool.

Before we left, Roderick's neighbor, Willy, walked over to Bonnie with paperwork for his dog, which was pregnant but healthy. The dog looked up at its owner and wagged its tail.

"You like this man, don't you? Yes, I can tell you do," Bonnie made kissing noises at the dog. "Glad to see these taken care of, these dogs. We don't always run across them that look this good."

"Yeah, these are my kids out here," Willy said proudly.

"Everybody had water. Everybody's fat. So Bonnie's happy," Bonnie smiled as we climbed back in the SUV. For now, her faith in humanity seemed to be restored and the festering ball of despondence retreated somewhere within her.

"I KNOW HOW TO PLAY THIS SHIT TOO"

As WE DROVE THROUGH THE NEXT NEIGHBORHOOD, we were welcomed by the crack of a gunshot.

"I don't know what they're doing," Bonnie said, adding that gunshots in Greene County are common.

We spotted a few doghouses and chained pit bulls near a trailer home, so Bonnie pulled off to talk to the owners.

Temperatures were in the nineties, and my shirt, which I had been wearing for days, was wetted with sweat and sunscreen. I replaced the battery in my camera and watched Bonnie rap on the door of the trailer home. Joe was seated in the back fussing with audio equipment. We exchanged mixed looks of worry and excitement in the rearview mirror.

Bonnie led the dog owner to his doghouses where a pregnant dog was on a chain so short that it couldn't retreat from the sun to its own shelter. Instead, it was digging a hole to unearth cool dirt and escape the heat. We watched them exchange words before Bonnie walked back to the SUV, grabbed her clipboard and told us to get out and take pictures of the pregnant dog while she discussed humane treatment with its owner. I was able to get a few shots before Bonnie called for us to get back in the car, urgency in her voice.

"Get in the house," a neighbor called to his kid playing in the street.

What the hell is going on, I thought, surveying the neighborhood as I swung my body into the SUV, and before I could buckle my seatbelt, Bonnie had the vehicle in gear.

The dog owner, she told us as we pulled out of the driveway, appeared to be on drugs and when she was trying to talk with him, he ran back inside the house. She was afraid he might have gone in to grab a weapon.

"Don't you just get tired of seeing crap like that?" Bonnie asked.

"I can't imagine," I said, feeling suddenly aware of the danger Bonnie encounters regularly.

"Well you can now," she said. "It'll make you crazy. I've told you, I'm not even the same person."

Bonnie's breathing grew fast. She sat upright with two hands gripping the wheel, scanning both sides of the road for suspicious activity. Since she began investigating animal cruelty in in 2007, the entire county knew what to do when her white SUV came crawling down their drive.

"This is common all through here. I wanna ... ughhh," Bonnie grunted. "I can't say what I want to do."

We watched as residents removed their animals from chains, hiding them in their homes or backyards and signifying the brutal truth that they knew what they were doing was inhumane or illegal. But to them, it was a game.

"Tell you what we might do, we're going to bluff them a little bit," Bonnie said. "We're going to go get us some coffee, then we're coming back. See, I know how to play this shit too. They're down here moving dogs and shit right now because everybody's on the block been calling 'em."

Bonnie cursed under her breath as she drove mockingly slow out of the neighborhood. We never did get coffee, and we never went back that night as planned, but it was on Bonnie's radar, in the pit of her stomach, festering. After we were comfortably home in Minnesota, she would return to that neighborhood alone. I just hoped she had a quick draw.

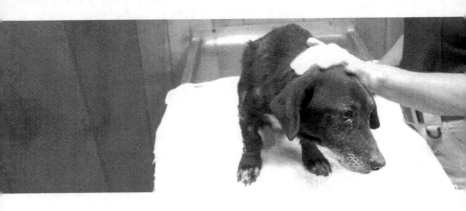

CANDY HEARTS

"JUST HOLD TIGHT, SOMETIMES I GET IN A HURRY," Bonnie laughed as she sped down a county road explaining to us how it's tough to canvass the entire county by herself. Most of the time, she doesn't make it 5 miles from her home without encountering animal abuse. On top of that, she receives tips from strangers and fields calls from the sheriffs department, which keeps her busy, but she's thankful for the help.

"We're going to go down this road. This could be interesting, I'm not sure," Bonnie smiled at me.

"I'm not a vigilante," she said. "I don't go in there like gangbusters."

As a religious woman, Bonnie views herself as a servant of the lord. She treats people with kindness, although she did admit to having a short fuse when it comes to ignorance.

"I'm a people person. I love people of all creeds and color, but the thing about it is, I do not like people to abuse their animals, and I guess I have zero tolerance for that," Bonnie said before spotting an old, mangy dog in front of a trailer home.

We followed her as she approached the dog, but it ran through a gap in the metal-sided base of the trailer home. Two young children opened the door and peeked out at us with interest. Bonnie asked them to get their parents.

A severely overweight woman filled the doorframe and Bonnie introduced herself in an upbeat, friendly manner.

"What happened to that little dog there, ma'am?" Bonnie asked.

"I don't know," the woman breathed heavy, adding that the dog had two litters of eight puppies.

"Where are they at?" Bonnie asked.

"They're somewhere around out here," the woman looked to the east, the west, then back at Bonnie.

"Right," Bonnie was annoyed that the woman didn't call someone to come get the dog and its eight puppies. Instead, she let them roam the neighborhood like squirrels.

The woman agreed to help Bonnie catch the dog, but when she had trouble walking down the front steps, Bonnie solicited her son's help instead. The boy squeezed out from behind his mom and shuffled down the stairs.

"Bandit!" the woman called out to the old dog, and it popped out from under the house, followed by two other adult dogs, one of which was also having multiple litters of puppies that were "somewhere around."

"Well ... ugh," Bonnie quickly became overwhelmed with the number of sickly, underweight dogs. "Let me see if I can get Bandit."

Another severely overweight gentleman appeared in the doorway. He teased Bandit out from underneath a truck so Bonnie could grab him. The dog tensed up and whimpered in fear.

"One of you guys quickly open the thing, because she's fixing to bite me," Bonnie moved fast toward the SUV.

Before leaving, we caught four stray puppies: one black, one brown, one tan and one mixed color. With five dogs in the vehicle, we thought we were done for the day, but Bonnie was just getting started.

Following the sound of barking dogs, we pulled into another driveway and wandered around to the backyard to find a shirtless teenage boy who had his shorts pulled down to mid-thigh, revealing his underwear.

Several pit bulls were chained to trees in the yard without water, and a female bulldog squinted at us through a growth of yellow puss surrounding its eyes. Bonnie walked the boy around the property and pointed out all the reasons why he was neglecting his animals.

They stood over the female bulldog that was covered in bite marks.

"Somebody's fought her. I don't know who fought her," Bonnie raised her clipboard and asked the boy for his first and last name.

To break the silence while Bonnie recorded information, I asked the boy if he knew people who fight dogs.

"No, not for real," he said.

Bonnie raised her head from the clipboard and laughed.

"You know they do it all around here, come on now. I know it, you bound to know it, we all know it," she laughed.

The boy's mother appeared at the back door of the house. Bonnie walked over to introduce herself, telling the woman that if her son didn't have the means to take the dog to the vet, she could sign it over to the county.

"Yeah, and I keep telling him, 'Boy why you keep getting these dogs and fighting them?'" the woman, who was speaking through a barely cracked open door to avoid my camera, made it clear that her son was a dog fighter.

The woman remained defensive, so Bonnie gave her two options: Release the dog to the custody of the humane society or have the Sheriff come out.

"Ok, take him," the woman surrendered.

The female bulldog occupied the final kennel in the vehicle, so we drove to the vet to have the dogs checked out. When I asked Bonnie how she pays for the vetting of so many animals, she told me they just put it on her tab, and when the money is there, the bills get paid.

The puppies were easily vetted within minutes, but the older mother dog—a Dachshund—was a different story: She had ticks, flees, arthritis, chronic hip luxation, several missing teeth, mange and skin burns.

"I would probably be inclined to put her to sleep," the vet said after rattling off the number of irreversible health problems plaguing the animal.

"The way I'm feeling about it is ... what's her quality of life going to be from this point on? I have arthritis, so I know what arthritis is like, this dog doesn't even have teeth," Bonnie rubbed the dog nervously and agreed that putting it down was the most humane option. She held its head up with one hand and patted it with the other while the vet sedated the dog so the euthanasia shot, which had to be poked through the dog's sensitive skin, wouldn't hurt.

"It's really sad, but that's what happens when there's a lack of care, guys," Bonnie said as the dog's eyes began to water. "It falls on the shoulders of people like me, the vet, the rescuer, and it really hurts.

"Love of a person or an animal is being able to let go. Because when we hang on to something that is suffering ... we hang on for who? Us? You have to think about that animal before yourself," Bonnie paused. She was wearing her sunglasses but I could tell she was tearing up. "This is really painful, I mean it rips my heart.

"Yeah baby dog, you rest in peace," she patted Bandit once more and swayed nervously, swallowing the lump in her throat before guiding us back to the SUV.

On Nov. 6, 2014, I was seated with my family around my grandmother's hospital bed. My grandma—who we refer to as Nanma—decided to stop all aggressive forms of treatment.

"We're waiting for someone to board the ship," my Nandad told a distant relative over the phone as he cried the sort of cry that remembers a lifetime of love.

Nanma's lungs were filling with fluid. She was, for lack of a more sensitive word, drowning. Her breathing became sporadic, and she wasn't able to speak a full sentence on a single breath.

"Happy," she said. "Happy tears."

She wanted us all to know that her tears were tears of joy. She lived a life of service to her church and was unwavering in her faith, which she held to strongly through her battle with cancer and up to those final moments.

Before the doctor increased her pain medication, which would relieve her suffering but ultimately end her life, Nanma lifted her frail arms and began pinching at the air like she was trying to pick berries from a high hanging branch.

"I see candy hearts," she said as she looked over her four children and the rest of her family flanking her hospital bed. Nanma chose to imagine her family surrounded by little candy hearts, floating and blinking with color like a sky full of stars, creating an aura of connective love.

I imagined the lettering on those candy hearts: *Be Kind; My Hero; Hold Me* and *Love*. Those were Nanma's final messages before she left us. She wanted to know that we all had the capacity to welcome love in our lives and to let our love bind us together as a family through tragedy and triumph ... to let it stand unwavering like her faith.

I will always wonder if that dog, in its final moments, saw little candy hearts around Bonnie. If, after a lifetime of abuse and neglect, it's faith in humanity was restored by a single act of love and kindness. If it's eyes watered with happiness.

After spending more 30 days in Alabama, I can't stop asking myself the same questions I asked while interviewing animal rescuers.

What is the solution?

What will it take to facilitate change?

Why this? Why that?

At the end of our trip, I had more questions than answers and more conflicting emotions. But, maybe the answer is simpler than its question. Maybe—to echo my Nanma's verdict on the great mystery of life—everything boils down to love.

Love grows in complexity with time and transcends its own purity. It carries with it depth and immeasurable weight. It's not easy: You can't form a task force around it or pen it in on a city council agenda. It must be practiced over time and experienced in variety. Maybe if our collective conscience shifts and allows for love to be more present in our vision of a better world, maybe then our companion animals will feel the residual effects.

THE ROAD HOME

B ONNIE AND I WERE SITTING IN HER BREEZEWAY drinking pina coladas. Her Rottweiler sat next to me begging to be scratched. We sat in silence, both reliving the day's events and trying hard to shake the stress of animal rescue.

I studied Bonnie as she leaned back and looked out over her kennels, where a dim, warm light shone from a telephone poll above. She was smiling, proud of the work she had done, and I tried to imagine a world without people like her. Not only people in the world of animal rescue, but also in other corners of society: people with passion and stamina. People with grit.

I imagined what a movie about Bonnie, directed by Clint Eastwood, would look and sound like: dark, yet mysteriously inspiring. The words of Charles Bukowski's famed poem, 'Roll the Dice,' came to mind:

"If you're going to try, go all the way. Otherwise, don't even start. This could mean losing girlfriends, wives, relatives and maybe even your mind. It could mean not eating for three or four days. It could mean freezing on a park bench. It could mean jail. It could mean derision. It could mean mockery—isolation. Isolation is the gift. All the others are a test of your endurance, of how much you really want to do it. And, you'll do it, despite rejection and the worst odds. And it will be better than anything else you can imagine. If you're going to try, go all the way. There is no other feeling like that. You will be alone with the gods,

and the nights will flame with fire. You will ride life straight to perfect laughter. It's the only good fight there is."

Joe was in the kennels playing with the puppies we rescued, which surprised me since he so fervently expressed his disdain for animals before our trip. Later, he would tell me that it was the animal rescuers who turned him. Seeing their plight and struggle made him feel more sympathy toward companion animals.

He was mostly interested in the blond puppy, which was the smallest of the bunch and having trouble getting her share of food and water. After picking the ticks out of her fur, Joe sent a picture of the puppy to his sister, who wanted to adopt it. We named her Charmin in reference to the soft toilet paper. In the end, Joe's sister was unable to keep Charmin, and since Joe grew attached to her, he decided to keep her himself, bringing full circle his transformation from the person who didn't understand the point of owning a pet to the person who now can't live without one.

Charmin was one of eight dogs we transported from Alabama to Minnesota. As a final gesture of gratitude, we revisited some of the rescuers we met along our trip, donating dog food and taking a few of their rescue dogs off their hands, vowing to stay in touch.

Transporting those dogs allowed us the privilege of experiencing a small facet of animal rescue and a narrow glimpse into the lives of the rescuers we followed. But after 1,000 miles of highway driving, we would have the luxury of dropping the dogs off at Cloquet Friends of Animals, where they would be properly vetted and put up for adoption. We would wash our hands clean and return to our normal lives.

We arrived in Duluth late at night and parked the RV in Joe's driveway, where I stayed with the dogs until Cloquet Friends of Animals opened the following morning. Duluth received a record rainfall that night, marking the worst flood the city had endured in 500 years.

Miraculously, there were no fatalities. Even a young boy who was sucked into a drainage pipe survived with minor cuts and bruises. The historic event, for me, marked the end of a life experience, the first time I ventured off on my own, toeing the line between journalism and activism.

It took time, but Duluth rebounded from the catastrophic flood. Neighbors helped neighbors, and city officials worked tirelessly to procure relief funding. There was a sense of togetherness everywhere we went. Free food and water at local churches for displaced residents and benefit concerts. The community was wounded as a whole and had the foresight to heal together.

The culture of animal cruelty in Alabama did not happen overnight, but like a deadly virus, manifested itself over time. I hope some day it, too, can leverage the power of community and heal itself in unity.

I try to make a conscious effort to remember my childhood. I pretend I'm standing at the end of our gravel driveway in Central Minnesota. Evening sunlight dapples, dragonflies pluck tiny insects from the sky and a cloud of dust hangs above the county road where a truck passed by minutes ago. I try to remember everything I can about that place: The smell of farm air pushing over a field of corn. The wide curve in the driveway, and the low spots that collected rain. The red bus shelter, the crickets, the small pond, the Native American sweat lodge hidden deep in the woods. I try to unbury those moments from my subconscious and allow them to breathe new life into me.

Years from now, I will look back on my life with a new nostalgia. I will place myself in Bonnie's SUV and feel beads of sweat roll down my cheeks. I will remember the creaking plastic of the RV as Joe and I bounced down interstate 65 toward Mobile. I will remember waking in Oak Mountain Campground, thumbing through my reporter's notebook. I will remember the cynicism I held toward the South. I will remember the dogs we saved and those that never stood a chance. By then, however, I will remember that place for what it was, because it will be different then. And thanks to the guardians of Alabama's companion animals, it will be better.

EPILOGUE

Travel Song #1
By David Cowardin

I met a North Georgia boy
with blood on his blade
He said a dog is a dog
and a spade is a spade
With his tongue moving fast
and his mind poorly made
He sat down at the bar
and he started to fade

> *I'm not black and white*
> *I live in the grey*
> *If I'm starting to fly*
> *I could blow away*
> *Like the start of tomorrow*
> *is ending today*
> *If I'm running from you*
> *then I can't help but stay*

I met a tough southern gal
with a thick southern drawl
She said the law is the law
but means nothing at all
With her future in hand
she'll be making the call
By ending the fight
she'll be taking the fall

> *I'm not quite a martyr*
> *though I'm learning to be*
> *And my passion runs deep*
> *like a bottomless sea*
> *But if I can't see the end*
> *then it's hard to agree*
> *On a line to be drawn*
> *between you and me*

I met a fun Southern Bell
with her Bible in hand
She said lay down your heart,
try taking a stand
With dirt on her dress
and her life fully planned
She'll be looking the part
but changing the brand

> *I've sent a few payers,*
> *never lived by the book*
> *I've shoved it aside*
> *but ill give it a look*
> *If I can't see it now*
> *at least I'll know what it took*
> *For you and me both*
> *to live in a nook*

I met a guy who escaped
with his body in tact
He said I've done my time
now I'm making a pact
To put it together
from what I had lacked
He said the odds are tough
but my agenda is backed

> *I've taken some hits*
> *and thrown a few too*
> *Comparatively*
> *my problems are few*
> *But behind the cards*
> *that we both drew*
> *There's a part of me*
> *that's a part of you*

I met a traveling man
on his way to the top
He said if you pass through enough
it can't hurt to stop
When your tires are burning

and the sun's 'bout to drop
He said try your luck here
but continue to shop

> *He's probably right*
> *about what he has found*
> *His wisdom is strong,*
> *his feet on the ground*
> *But there's something behind me*
> *I'm hearing the sound*
> *If it's coming from you*
> *then I'll turn right around*

ABOUT THE AUTHOR

Author, filmmaker, fly fisherman, and doggy Dad.

David is an author and award-winning photojournalist living
in Duluth, Minnesota. He founded the production company,
Lola Visuals, where he directs and edits humanitarian video
campaigns. His work has provoked social change and inspired
community dialogue about animal welfare, environmental
sustainability, mental illness awareness and disability education.

David is a 20 Under 40 award recipient in Duluth where the
community has recognized his work as important and transfor-
mative. He manages the outdoor news website, Duluth Outdoors,
which helped earn his city the title of Best Outdoor Town in 2014.

Recent projects include: *Roots of Rescue*, *Call Me Mental*
and *The Awareness Campaign*.

Made in the USA
Middletown, DE
20 May 2016